A TOUR OF QUFU
THE HOMETOWN OF
CONFUCIUS

游访孔庙孔府孔林

Yang Zhaoming

Better Link Press

This book is edited and designed by the Editorial Committee of *Cultural China* series

Managing Directors: Wang Youbu, Xu Naiqing

Editorial Director: Wu Ying

Editors: Jennifer Wilde, Yang Xinci

Assistant Editor: Jiang Junyan

Text: Yang Zhaoming

Translation: Qiu Maoru

Cover Design: Wang Wei

Interior Design: Yuan Yinchang, Hu Bin

Cover and Backcover Images: Quanjing, Getty Images

ISBN: 978-1-60220-305-1

Address any comments about *Travel through the Middle Kingdom: A Tour of Qufu — the Hometown of Confucius* to:

Better Link Press

99 Park Ave

New York, NY 10016

USA

or

Shanghai Press and Publishing Development Company

F 7 Donghu Road, Shanghai, China (200031)

Email: comments_betterlinkpress@hotmail.com

Computer typeset by Yuan Yinchang Design Studio, Shanghai

Printed in China by Shanghai Donnelley Printing Co. Ltd.

1   2   3   4   5   6   7   8   9   10

The temple, cemetery and family mansion of Confucius, the great philosopher, politician and educator of the 6th-5th centuries B.C., are located at Qufu, in Shandong Province. Built to commemorate him in 478 B.C., the temple has been destroyed and reconstructed over the centuries; today it comprises more than 100 buildings. The cemetery contains Confucius' tomb and the remains of more than 100,000 of his descendants. The small house of the Kong family developed into a gigantic aristocratic residence, of which 152 buildings remain. The Qufu complex of monuments has retained its outstanding artistic and historic character due to the devotion of successive Chinese emperors over more than 2,000 years.

—World Heritage Council of the UNESCO

CONTENTS

CONTENTS

Foreword

China is known as *Zhong Guo* or Middle Kingdom in Chinese. This term originates from the 10th Century BC when the Zhou Dynasty was defending itself from encroaching barbarians. The Middle Kingdom then stretched from the modern day province of Jiangsu in the east to Sichuan in the west, from Hebei in the north-east and to parts of Gansu in the north-west. The Middle Kingdom was not a nation-state, but the assertion of a unified, highly developed and centralized culture. Cultural relics and artifacts, as well as historical documents from this period, demonstrate how technologically advanced the Middle Kingdom was. From its uniquely sophisticated script to its metallurgical discoveries, the Middle Kingdom had no rivals in the Far East. Silk, magnificent bronzes and jades and Chinese characters all attest to the fact that the Middle Kingdom was the center of civilization. It has maintained its cultural supremacy for thousands of years, its influence spreading to Japan and Korea, and reaching all the way to Vietnam and Indonesia.

The term Middle Kingdom has since come to represent one of the oldest civilizations in the world. The Great Wall of China, the Terracotta Warriors of Xi'an and the Forbidden City are just a few of the sites that introduce visitors to the magnificent history and culture of the Middle Kingdom. A walk through Suzhou Gardens, a hike through Yellow Mountain, or a boat ride down the Three Gorges will offer the visitor a more leisurely expedition. Traveling through the Middle Kingdom may sometimes be a challenge, but is always rewarding.

This series aims to offer an in-depth look at some of these famous locations, and to give the discerning traveler detailed descriptions as well as a thorough historical and cultural background. With beautiful illustrations and photographs, you will find our Travel through the Middle Kingdom books a most trustworthy companion, and a useful introduction to the wonders of China.

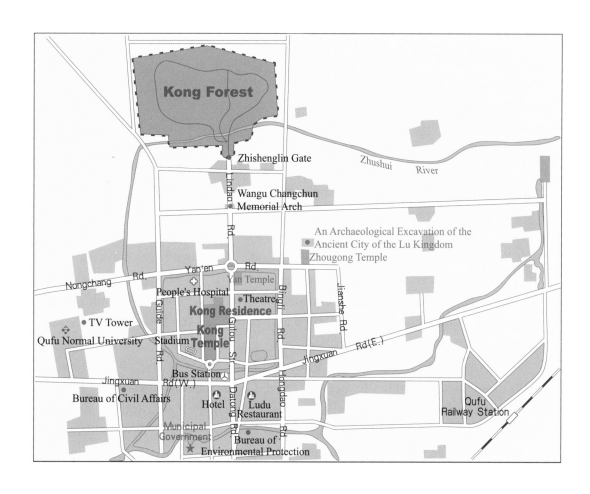

Places of Interest in Qufu

Advice for Travelling in Qufu

The Best Seasons for Visiting Qufu

Located in the Shandong Peninsula, Qufu has a continental monsoon climate with a great deal of sunlight. It boasts four distinct seasons: a dry and windy spring, a hot and rainy summer, a mild and cool autumn and a dry and cold winter with little snow. All four seasons are suitable for visiting Qufu. However, the months between March and November are peak tourist seasons.

Information
Admission:
Kong Temple: RMB90 (from March to November)
          RMB80 (from December to February)
Kong Residence: RMB60 (from March to November)
          RMB50 (from December to February)
Kong Forest: RMB40 (from March to November)
          RMB30 (from December to February)
Through Ticket: RMB150
Opening Hours: 8 am to 6 pm

Tips
• Recommended itinerary: Kong Temple—Kong Residence—A tour of Kong Forest by horse-drawn carriage (On the way you can visit the Yan Temple and the Wangu Changchun Memorial Arch.)
• September 28 is the birthday of Kongzi. From September 26 to October 10 every year the China Festival of Kongzi International Culture is held in Qufu. During the festival great events such as a sacrificial rite and music and dancing performances are exhibited in front of the Dacheng Hall in Kong Temple.

Delicious Foods & Delicacies
Stir-fried lake shrimps and mung bean sprouts
Legend has it that Emperor Qianlong displayed a poor appetite when he came to offer sacrifices to Kongzi in Kong Temple. The chef of Kong Residence grasped a handful of mung bean sprouts and stir-fried them together with some lake shrimps. The yellow-and-white dish was so inviting that Emperor Qianlong's appetite was roused. The emperor named this dish "jin gou gua yin tiao" (silver noodles hanging on gold hooks). Ever since then, this dish has been served in the banquets held in Kong Residence.

Ginkgo Dish
Kongzi encouraged his son Kong Li to study *The Book of Songs* and *the Rites* by saying: "You don't know how to talk if you don't study *The Book* of Songs. You don't know how to get along with the world or conduct yourself in society if you don't study *The Rites*." Kongzi's offspring were proud of being members of a family of poetry and rites. The Duke of Yansheng Kong Zhi, Kongzi's descendant of the 53rd generation, built the Poetry and Rites Hall to honour this event. There were two hardy and straight ginkgo trees. When the fruit was ripe, ginkgos were used to make a dish and it was named "shi li yin xing" (poetry and rites ginkgo dish). This amber-looking light food has become one of the traditional dishes served in the banquets held in Kong Residence.

Magic Duck
One day, the chef of Kong Fanpo, Kongzi's descendant of the 74th generation, cooked a steamed duck. The delicious duck was fatty but not greasy. When Kong Fanpo asked the chef how he cooked the dish, the chef said, "When I put the duck into a steamer, I started to burn an incense stick. When the incense was burned up, the duck was done." Kong Fanpo was so amazed by this that he said, "What a magic duck!" Ever since then the "magic duck" has also become one of the delicacies featuring in the banquets held in Kong Residence.

Introduction

Oriental culture, and especially Chinese culture, is noted for its unique style and charm in the treasure house of world civilizations. The colourful and traditional Chinese culture is composed of a distinctive character-formed language, voluminous classical works, marvellous art and literature, profound philosophy and religion, deep moral principles and ethics, and superb garden architecture. In China, the most concrete embodiment of traditional Chinese culture is Qufu, a city of historical and cultural value that is world renowned for the Kongzi Museum, Kong Temple, Kong Residence and Kong Forest.

Qufu is the birth place of traditional Chinese culture and its manifestation—Kongzi, the founder of Confucianism. Kongzi, also known as Confucius or Kongfuzi, is the most famous philosopher and educator of ancient China. Proud of being the birth place of Kongzi, an eminent historical personage in world culture, Qufu also boasts a host of physical and historical qualities.

Geographically, Qufu is situated in southern Shandong Province with the Taishan Mountain to its north, Zoucheng and Tengzhou to its south, Mount Nishan and Mount Fangshan to its east and an expanse of fertile land to its west. The city is surrounded by the Zhushui River, the Sishui River and the Yishui River. It has a prime location which seldom experiences natural disasters such as drought, flooding, typhoons or earthquakes. Thanks to its favourable geographic conditions, Qufu became a political, economic and cultural center of China at an early stage. In ancient times Shaohao, leader of the Yi people, made Qufu his capital. And during the Zhou Dynasty, the city of Qifu was made the capital of the Lu Kingdom where good governance and the advancement of culture and education prevailed for around 800 years. The Shaohao Mausoleum, the Temple of the Duke of Zhou and the ancient city of the Lu Kingdom are historical witnesses to the development of the city. The unique cultural and geographical environment of Qufu combined with the inertia of centuries-old politics and philosophical ideals combined to give birth to Kongzi, an eminent and influential person in world history and culture.

Kongzi lived in an era of profound social upheaval, ideological collision and cultural exchange. Such a social and cultural atmos-phere afforded Kongzi ample opportunity to draw historical nourishment and develop his ideology. Throughout his whole life, Kongzi was diligent and eager to learn. By studying and summarizing his historical and cultural heritage, he was led to deconstruct and question his observations, thus gaining an insight into how society worked. As a result, Kongzi put forth a detailed theory about his ideal society. Concurrently, he took up an official career and travelled to many states. Everywhere Kongzi travelled he set up private schools, trained talented people and spread his values and ideals. Gradually, Confucianism as a school of thought was founded with the culture, etiquette and music of the Zhou Dynasty and the Lu Kingdom as its base.

During the Period of the Warring States, Confucianism was regarded as the most renowned of all the schools of thought. A fierce rivalry between the other various schools of thought in the Spring and Autumn Period and the Period of the Warring States served to widen the influence of Confucianism and enhance its scholastic status. In the middle period of the Western Han Dynasty, Emperor Wu adopted the proposal put forward by Dong Zhongshu to "pay supreme tribute to Confucianism while banning all other schools of thought". As a result, Confucianism—the

Contention of numerous schools of thought in the Spring and Autumn Period, and the Period of the Warring States.
Contention became common practice in the Spring and Autumn Period, and the Period of the Warring States. That was the reflection of social reform in ideology. With the emergence of various schools of thought—Confucian School, Taoist School, Mohist School, School of Logicians, Legalist School, *Yin-Yang* School, School of Political Strategists and School of Agriculturalists—fierce contention in the political and academic fields was started. The contention of numerous schools of thought played a great role in promoting the cultural and academic development in China.

ideological system of Kongzi—was established as the dominant way of thought of the feudal society. Influenced gradually and imperceptibly by the ideals of Kongzi for over 2,000 years, the Chinese people have taken Confucianism as a guiding principle in their thinking and behaviour, and even as a benchmark for regulating family life and social morality. Confucianism has also exerted a great influence on many other countries and regions in the East.

For the purpose of showing respect to Kongzi, emperors of various dynasties conferred one title after another upon him. In the late period of the Western Han Dynasty Kongzi was awarded the title of "Duke of Xuanni". The titles of "Prince of Wenxuan" and "Accomplished Sage Prince of Wenxuan" were conferred upon him in the Tang and Yuan Dynasties respectively. In the early period of the Qing Dynasty, Kongzi was esteemed as the "model teacher for all ages". Even his offspring of lineal descent were held in high esteem. Emperor Gaozu of the Han Dynasty bestowed the title of "Prince of Fengsi (in charge of offering sacrifices)" upon them. The hereditary title "the Duke of Yansheng" was granted in the Northern Song Dynasty and lasted until the founding of the Republic of China. Rulers of various dynasties made continued efforts to expand the temple of sacrificial offerings to Kongzi and to mete out preferential treatment to his offspring. With the passage of generations, Qufu has become a city with precious historical and cultural heritage. Its most notable buildings are Kong Temple, where sacrifices were offered to Kongzi; the Kong Residence, where his offspring of lineal

Dong Zhongshu

Dong Zhongshu was a great thinker in the middle period of the Western Han Dynasty. He proposed to Emperor Wu that only Confucianism should be advocated and his proposal was accepted. He specialized in the study of *Spring and Autumn Annals with Commentaries by Gongyang Gao* and had a great impact on the society and on the development of Confucian classics. He held the idea that heaven dominates nature and human society and the emperor is the representative of heaven on earth. Therefore, he advocated that the power of the emperor is delegated by heaven itself.

A Glimpse at Kong Forest

descent lived; and Kong Forest, where Kongzi and his offspring are buried. Qufu become well known as "a sacred city in the East".

Kong Temple is Kongzi's former home. Liu Bang, Emperor Gaozu of the Han Dynasty, paid homage to Kongzi here. During the reign of Emperor Huan of the Eastern Han Dynasty, the Prime Minister Han Chi used public funds to renovate Kong Temple, thus turning it into a government-established temple. Emperor Taizong of the Tang Dynasty issued an imperial edict that temples to honour Kongzi be erected in the capital city and other places all over the country. He gave special orders to build Queli Kong Temple in Qufu, making this the biggest and most elite temple—the "model of all Kong temples" and the "main temple to offer sacrifices to Kongzi" from the whole country. Kong Temple symbolizes the distinguished position Kongzi and Confucianism attained in ancient China. The change in status of Kong Temple bears witness to the development of official ideology and the evolution of orthodox doctrines of thinking and culture. Kong Temple is the epitome and symbol of traditional Chinese culture.

A typical patriarchal agrarian society, characteristic of Chinese society, lasted until modern times. The Kong Family was looked upon as the most typical representation of such a society. The 2,400 years between Kongzi and Kong Decheng, a direct descendent of the 77th generation from the paternal line, witnessed a unique social and cultural phenomenon: the procreation of a large family with strict rules and regulations, and a meticulous system of management which epitomized the development of the whole society. As the physical carrier of this phenomenon, the Kong Residence played the role of paying homage to Kongzi and carrying forward Confucianism. Different parts of the residence symbolized different social positions. There was a demarcation between the front part and the back part of the residence with the former for external business and the latter for domestic life. Even the use of the front or side doors signified the proper order of seniority. In the exuberant Kong Forest, Kongzi has rested in peace for over 2,400 years. With continual extension, Kong Forest today covers an area of more than 180 hectares. Kongzi's countless offspring have been buried around him—always in order of seniority.

Culture is at once both tangible and intangible. As the physical embodiment of Chinese temple culture, ancient documentation culture, gardening culture and tomb culture, Kong Temple, Kong Residence and the Kong Forest belong to tangible culture. Intangible culture refers to the belief systems and the ideologies of the people. These are the founding thoughts of the cultural environment of Qufu, where, as Su Dongpo, a literary giant in the Song Dynasty, pointed out in his poem, all the people there formed a good habit of reading. Qufu was permeated with this traditional intangible Chinese culture. Kong Temple, the Kong Residence and the Kong Forest were in the first group of major preserved cultural relics announced by the State Council in 1961. Qufu was listed as one of the first group of 24 famous historical and cultural cities announced by the State Council in 1982. Again in 1994, Kong Temple, the Kong Residence and the Kong Forest were placed on the UN list of the World Cultural Heritage Sites by UNESCO in 1994.

Kong Temple
—China's No.1 Temple

Kong Temple is abundant in significant stone tablets and towering ancient trees outside and complete with sacrificial vessels, musical instruments and dancing implements inside. Qufu's Kong Temple is the oldest museum in the world and as "China's No.1 Temple" is true to its name.

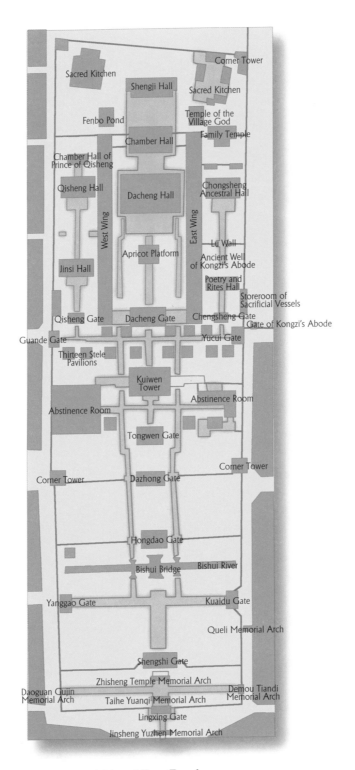

A Map of Kong Temple

If you were to look at Qufu from above, you would find a solemn building with a yellow tiled roof and grey brick walls among the green trees. This is none other than Kong Temple itself. To the east stands Kong Residence, a huge residential compound of classical style, within which there are nine rows of courtyard houses. The Kong Forest is situated two kilometres north of Kong Temple and Kong Residence. With an area of over 200 hectares, the thick forest is teeming with exuberant ancient trees. As soon as you arrive in Qufu, you'll sense a strong flavour of Confucian culture. The harmonious merge of modern civilization and traditional culture presents a beautiful picture. As the hometown of Kongzi and Confucianism, Qufu is full of solemn, ancient and elegant cultural relics dedicated to Kongzi and Confucianism, thus creating a sacred atmosphere. This abundant cultural heritage is due to one sacred personage—Kongzi.

Kongzi—an Eminent Personage in Cultural Circles of the World

In today's world, many people still believe we should seek wisdom and guidance from the historical figure of Kongzi in order to prosper in the 21st century. Let's appreciate the enduring and all-embracing wisdom

Portrait of Kongzi

of Kongzi by looking at his life and touring Kong Temple, Kong Residence and the Kong Forest one after another.

A Biographical Sketch of Kongzi

Kongzi was born in 551 BC in the Lu Kingdom—a state well known for rites and folk songs. His forefathers were noble men and his father, Shuliang, was a famous warrior in the Lu Kingdom. His father died when Kongzi was just a little boy. Kongzi grew up in Queli of Qufu, the capital of the Lu Kingdom, and was nurtured by the strong cultural atmosphere there. He began to engage all his energy in his studies at the age of 15. He started to teach at the age of 30. It is said that Kongzi had altogether over 3,000 students, of whom 72 talented disciples became accomplished persons. In his early fifties, Kongzi took up the official posts of Prime Minister of Lu, Minister of Public Works and Minister of Justice in succession. As the Lu Kingdom was in political turmoil, Kongzi found it difficult to pursue and realize his lofty aspirations. Accompanied by his disciples Yan Hui, Zilu and Zigong, 55-year-old Kongzi started to lead a nomadic lifestyle, wandering from one state to another. During those 14 years he exerted all possible efforts to propagate his ideology and doctrines, which, however, were not valued in some states. Kongzi returned to the Lu Kingdom at the age of 68, where he was looked up to as "the First Senior of the State". He devoted his remaining years to education and documentation. In 479 BC, Kongzi died of illness at the age of 73.

The Thought and Doctrines of Kongzi

As an old Chinese saying goes, "the mastery of half *The Analects of Confucius* suffices to rule the country". Though exaggerated, the remarks reflect the important role of this book. *The Analects of Confucius* gave expression to the erudite thought and doctrines of Kongzi.

With "benevolence" at the core of his thought and doctrines, Kongzi described its meaning as "care for others". That means "do not do to others what you would not have them do to you". If one wishes to establish oneself, one should help others to do likewise. This can be understood as the principle of "loyalty and forbearance". The all-embracing concept of "benevolence" as the love shown to others, including one's family, society and nature, is the point from which one can explore the path one should follow in life, and explore ways of solving social problems. This is the general

The Analects of Confucius

The Analects of Confucius, one of the great Confucian classics, records the words and deeds of Kongzi and his disciples. This book is a collection of the typical notes Kongzi's students took while listening to his lectures on morality and education. This book serves as the main source book for the study of Kongzi thought.

program of Confucian world outlook—an outlook on life and values.

Kongzi advocated the "rule of virtue" as his political logic. According to him, "benevolence", as the general principle of Confucianism, is the highest moral standard. Starting from "benevolence", Kongzi proposed a series of successive moral standards, such as righteousness, rites, knowledge, faith and valor. Politically speaking, "benevolence" means "rule of virtue" and "rule of education" and is opposed to tyrannical governance and the death penalty. Kongzi was against overworking the proletariat and in favour of enriching individuals and respecting their dignity.

"In education, there should be no distinction of social status." This is the defining sentiment of his doctrines on education which targeted the common people. Kongzi was the first person to foster an atmosphere of private lecturing and to advocate "no distinction of social status in education", thus ending the nobility's monopolization of education and offering the working classes an opportunity to access education. Kongzi accumulated rich experience in his decades of teaching practice and formulated a systematic theory of education, such as "teaching a student according to his or her aptitude", "teaching with skill and patience" and "teaching with tireless zeal". In addition, Kongzi re-edited such classical works as *The Book of Songs*, *Collection of Ancient Texts*, *The Rites* and *The Book of Music* and used them as teaching materials. He wrote *The Spring and Autumn Annals* and *Commentaries on Changes*. They have become part of China's precious historical and cultural heritage.

Kongzi was a wise and kind-hearted man. He hoped that his doctrines would be accepted by the wider population and that his ideal of a harmonious society would be realized. Kongzi dedicated his whole life to advocating his doctrines. This in itself is a demonstrable manifestation of his respect for culture and his spirit of diligence and enterprise.

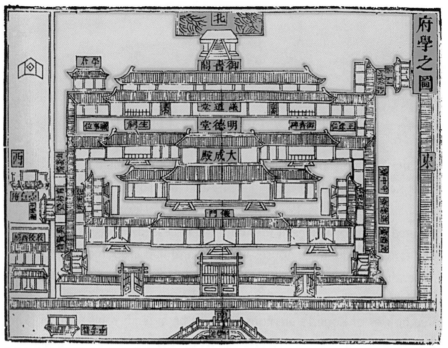

Prefectural School of Jiankang in the Southern Song Dynasty

Respectful Temple Culture

Kong Temple in Qufu is undoubtedly the largest and oldest of all the Confucian temples in the world. Kong Temple in Qufu, the Imperial Palace in Beijing and the Mountain Resort in Chengde, Hebei Province are known as China's three largest ancient architectural complexes. This age-old and well-preserved complex of oriental architecture serves as a comprehensive museum of history, culture, carving, painting and calligraphy. Kong Temple is abundant in significant stone tablets and towering ancient trees outside and is complete with sacrificial vessels, musical instruments and dancing implements inside. The Kong Temple in Qufu is the oldest museum in the world and as "China's No. 1 Temple" is true to its name.

History of Kong Temple

Kong Temple was established in 478 BC, a year after Kongzi's death. While Kongzi was alive, the Duke of Ai in the Lu Kingdom often asked him for advice. He was so grieved by the death of Kongzi, that he himself delivered a memorial speech to mourn the deceased. He issued an imperial edict to rebuild the three houses where Kongzi had lived into a temple. The clothes, hats, musical instruments, carriages and books used by Kongzi were stored there and his descendants could pay homage to him here. These three houses of Kongzi's are considered to be an embryonic form of Kong Temple. Over time, Kong Temple was renovated again and again and the giant complex of buildings we are familiar with today began to take shape during the Ming and Qing Dynasties. The largest renovation was started in 1724, the second year of the reign of Emperor Yongzheng of the Qing Dynasty. As many as 157,000 taels of silver were spent on this six-year construction project. Upon completion, the completely renovated Kong Temple assumed it's present-day dimensions.

A Tour of Kong Temple

The moment you step onto the sacred land of Qufu, you will be compelled to visit Kong Temple, a huge and imposing ancient temple, where you can pay your respects to Kongzi and savour the profound

Thousand-feet-high Palace Walls

theories of Confucianism. The following guide will introduce the highlights of Kong Temple.

Prelude

Immeasurably High Palace Walls

When you drive from Qufu Railway Station along State Highway No. 327, you'll catch sight of a magnificent and imposing complex of ancient buildings at the northern end of the "sacred way". You'll be immediately attracted by the four big red characters— 万仞宫墙 *wan ren gong qiang*, or Ten-Thousand-*Ren*-High Palace Walls. This is the starting point of your tour of Kong Temple.

Jinsheng Yuzhen Memorial Arch

The saying "wan ren gong qiang" is quoted from *The Analects of Confucius*. It is recorded that an official in the Lu Kingdom said that Zigong, a disciple of Kongzi, was more learned than Kongzi. In reply, Zigong made a comparison. He said, "One's learning is like a palace wall. My wall is only shoulder-high, so everyone can see inside my palace. My teacher's wall is several *ren* high. If you can't find the door, you are unable to enjoy

Layout of Kong Temple

Kong Temple was modelled on an imperial palace with nine courtyards. The left and right areas of the temple, standing on either side of a 1000-metre-long central line, are symmetrical in structure. Composed of 104 buildings and 466 rooms, it covers an area of 9.6 hectares. The structure includes one tower, one platform, two wings, two halls, three ancestral temples, five palace halls, 17 stele pavilions and 54 gates and memorial arches.

neither the splendour of the palace nor the beauty of colourful houses inside the wall." The character "ren" means 7 or 8 feet in ancient Chinese. Zigong compared Kongzi's profound and unfathomable learning to "high walls". The later generation increased "several *ren*" to "ten thousand *ren*" to praise the depth of Kongzi's thought.

Jinsheng Yuzhen Memorial Arch

When you pass through *wan ren gong qiang*, you'll come across the first stone memorial arch—Jinsheng Yuzhen Memorial Arch.

The saying "jin sheng yu zhen" is quoted from *Mengzi* (or *Mencius*). In ancient China, musical performances usually began with the ringing of a bell (*jin sheng*) and ended with the hitting of a jade percussion instrument (*yu zhen*). Therefore, "jin sheng yu zhen" means the whole process of a musical performance. Mengzi used this figure of speech to illustrate Kongzi's thought, which, he believed, was a comprehensive combination of the wisdom and knowledge of all his predecessors. This memorial arch was erected in the front part of Kong Temple to highlight Kongzi's scope and versatility.

Unique Charm of Gates

The solemn and imposing manner of Kong Temple was initially revealed by the "dismounting tablet" in front of Kong Temple. After you walk

Mengzi (Mencius)
The book has become one of the important Confucian classics. Compiled by Mengzi and his disciple Wan Zhang, the book records the political activities and words of Mengzi. *Mengzi* serves as the main source book for the study of Mengzi and his thought.

Dismounting Tablet

through the Jinsheng Yuzhen Memorial Arch, you will be faced with the Lingxing Gate. On both sides of the gate stand tablets which read "All officials and others are required to dismount here", hence the "dismounting tablet". In ancient times, any official, whether high-ranking or not, was required to dismount from his horse or sedan chair when he entered or passed by the Kong Temple. This was considered appropriate behaviour and showed respect for Kongzi.

Looking through the Jinsheng Yuzhen Memorial Arch inside the temple, you will find a perfectly straight path leading from one gate to another. The courtyards in between the gates are decorated with ancient trees and fragrant grasses. The red walls along both sides are dotted with several side doors. Beautiful egrets are perched on the imposing cypresses or flying above them. This scene adds to the deep, serene and solemn atmosphere of the temple.

Lingxing Gate

Walking along the path, you are greeted by one vermilion gate after another. The inscriptions on every gate in famous personages' calligraphy either depict Confucian thought or sing Kongzi's praises. You can savour the essence of Kongzi's life and thoughts while touring these history-steeped gates.

Lingxing Gate

The front gate of Kong Temple was first built as a wooden structure in the early Ming Dynasty and was renovated and rebuilt into one with stone pillars and iron beams in 1754 (in the 19th year of the reign of Emperor Qianlong of the Qing Dynasty). The four pillars are carved with auspicious clouds and at the top of each pillar there is a sculpture of a furious heavenly warrior in a seated position. Twelve *fayue* (column heads commending meritorious service) with dragon-head design are cast on the iron beams. The architrave

Taihe Yuanqi Memorial Arch

is divided into two parts: the top one is carved with decorative patterns while the bottom one is inscribed with three characters: "ling xing men" in the handwriting of Emperor Qianlong of the Qing Dynasty and accompanied by his seal. "Ling xing" was regarded in ancient times as a star in charge of teaching. The front gate of Kong Temple was so named as to compare the great educator Kongzi to the star on earth. People in the past would worship the star before they offered sacrifices to Heaven. The choice of this name for the front gate of Kong Temple was intended to encourage people to show as much respect to Kongzi as to Heaven.

Taihe Yuanqi Memorial Arch

Behind the Lingxing Gate is the Taihe Yuanqi Memorial Arch. The memorial arch was built in 1544 (in the 23rd year of the reign of Emperor Jiajing of the Ming Dynasty) and the four characters "tai he yuan qi" were written by Zeng Xian, the Imperial Inspector in Shandong. The Chinese

Zhisheng Temple Memorial Arch

word "tai he" means "universal peace and harmony", while "yuan qi" means "vitality". In the minds of the ancient people, all creatures on earth were nurtured by harmony and vitality. People likened the Kongzi doctrines to harmony and vitality in order to show the close relationship between Confucian thought and people's social beliefs.

Zhisheng Temple Memorial Arch

To the north of the Taihe Yuanqi Memorial Arch stands Zhisheng Temple Memorial Arch. The temple was originally called Xuansheng Temple and was renamed Zhisheng Temple in 1729 (the 7th year of the reign of Emperor

Yongzheng of the Qing Dynasty). Xuansheng and Zhisheng were honorifics bestowed upon Kongzi after his death. Zhisheng means "the greatest sage, Kongzi". As Confucianism was very highly esteemed in feudal society, the well-known scholars advocating Confucianism were respectfully called "sages" (*sheng*). For example, Duke of Zhou, Mengzi (Mencius), Yan Hui, Zengzi and Zisi were termed *yuan* (first) *sheng*, *ya* (second) *sheng*, *fu* (duplicate) *sheng*, *zong* (great master) *sheng* and *shu* (narrate) *sheng* respectively. This depicts their being held in great esteem as a result of their outstanding contributions to the practice and promotion of Confucianism.

Shengshi Gate

Behind Zhisheng Temple is the second gate of Kong Temple, the Shengshi Gate. The gate was built in the Ming Dynasty. Standing on one-metre-high steps with three archways, the gate structure looks not unlike a citadel. It is of typical ancient Chinese architectural style with upturned eaves and green glazed tiles. The Chinese word "shengshi", quoted from

Duke of Zhou

The Duke of Zhou was a politician and thinker during the late period of the Shang Dynasty and the early period of the Zhou Dynasty. The Duke of Zhou assisted King Wu in overthrowing the Shang Dynasty and founding the Western Zhou Dynasty. After King Wu died, he worked for King Cheng. As a high-ranking official for seven years, he played an important role in quashing rebellions and stabilizing the country's governance. He advocated respect to heaven, protection of all people, high moral principles and caution in punishment. All this contributed to the forming of Confucian doctrines. He was therefore called "yuansheng" (first sage) by people of later ages.

Yan Hui

Yan Hui, courtesy name Ziyuan, was born in the Lu Kingdom at the end of the Spring and Autumn Period. He was Kongzi's favourite student. Though coming from a poor family, Yan Hui was happy to lead a simple and virtuous life. He never tired of learning and showed great respect to his teacher. He was well-known for his moral integrity. Kongzi praised him for his virtuous talent. Unfortunately, he died in his prime. He was esteemed as "fusheng" during the reign of Emperor Jiajing of the Ming Dynasty.

Right: Shengshi Gate

Hongdao Gate

Dazhong Gate

Mengzi, was used to describe Kongzi as a sage who could well adapt himself to a range of circumstances, thus becoming an educator and philosopher required by the society and the times. The naming of the gate was approved by Emperor Yongzheng and the tablet was written by Emperor Qianlong.

Hongdao Gate

After passing the Shengshi Gate, you'll find yourself in a bright open courtyard with densely grown ancient cypresses and a soft carpet of green grass. In the northern part of the courtyard, there is a winding stream the colour of jade, which is spanned by the three-arched Bishui (literally, "jade water") Bridge. The carved stone balustrades of the bridge are as intricate as those of the Jinshui ("gold water") Bridge in Beijing. The construction of the bridge began during the reign of Emperor Hongwu of the Ming Dynasty. The bridge was built in 1504 (the 17th year of the reign of Emperor Hongzhi of the Ming Dynasty) and renovated in the Qing Dynasty. To the north of the Bishui Bridge lies the Hongdao Gate.

The Hongdao Gate is the third principal gate of Kong Temple. The name of the gate was chosen by Emperor Yongzheng of the Qing Dynasty in 1729 (the 7th year of his reign). The Chinese word "hong dao", quoted from *The Analects of Confucius*, means that people can promote and popularize fine traditional virtues.

Dazhong Gate

To the north of the Hongdao Gate is the Dazhong Gate. This fourth principal gate was actually the front gate of Kong Temple before the Song Dynasty. Standing at a five doors wide, this green-glazed-tile-covered gate is actually narrower than the Hongdao Gate. The gate was rebuilt during the reign of Emperor Hongzhi of the Ming Dynasty and what we see today is the result of reconstruction during the Qing Dynasty. On either side of the gate stands a green-glazed-tile watchtower. Together with the two matching ones on both sides of the north wall of Kong Temple, the watchtowers were built in 1331 (the 2nd year of the reign of Emperor Zhishun of the Yuan Dynasty) for the purpose of making Kong Temple look as imposing as the imperial palace. They were renovated during the Ming and Qing Dynasties. The gate was originally called "zhong he men (gate)" and later renamed "da zhong men (gate)". The renaming of the gate was intended to emphasize the doctrine of the mean advocated by Kongzi and Confucianism.

Tongwen Gate

Behind the Dazhong Gate is the Tongwen Gate. The Tongwen Gate was

Tongwen Gate

the main entrance of Kong Temple in the Song Dynasty. With a width of five rooms and a depth of two rooms, this gate is independent of any walls. You will be attracted by its yellow glazed tiles and beautiful coloured patterns. The gate was called "can tong men (gate)" in the early Qing Dynasty and was renamed "tong wen men (gate)" after the reign of Emperor Shunzhi.

Kongzi made outstanding contributions to the development of Chinese culture by founding Kongzi doctrines, popularizing education, cultivating

The *Doctrine of the Mean*

The *Doctrine of the Mean* was originally an article written by Kongzi's grandson Kong Zisi and collected in *The Rites*. Later, Zhu Xi selected this article and made it into an independent book of the four major Confucian classics. "Zhong" means "impartial" while "yong" means "ordinary". Kongzi proposed that the doctrine of the mean be regarded as the moral principles people should adopt in their words and deeds. Zisi further expounded this theory and advocated "harmony" as the highest standard of moral conduct and the fundamental order of all things on earth. With the development of this theory, the doctrine of the mean has become a basic approach adopted by Confucians to understand the world and address social life.

talented people and managing historical documents. His contributions had a great impact on different aspects of Chinese society and especially on the spread of Chinese culture from generation to generation. The Chinese word "tong wen", quoted from *The Doctrine of the Mean*, means the pursuance of cultural unification. The fifth gate of Kong Temple was so named to eulogize Kongzi's brilliant contributions to the development of Chinese culture.

Splendour of Side Doors

The unique and splendid architecture of Kong Temple is evident even in the construction of its side doors. Most of the six spacious courtyards in front of the Dacheng Gate each have a pair of matching side doors. The naming of these side doors is meaningful and displays the imposing manner of Kong Temple and the profundity of Kongzi thought.

The Demou Tiandi Memorial Arch, the Daoguan Gujin Memorial Arch
A pair of side doors are located to the east and west of the first courtyard

Demou Tiandi Memorial Arch

Daoguan Gujin Memorial Arch

and called "de mou tian di fang (memorial arch)" and "dao guan gu jin fang (memorial arch)" respectively. This pair of side doors was built of wood in 1415 (in the 13th year of the reign of Emperor Yongle of the Ming Dynasty). The three-room, four-pillar, five-story memorial arches are supported by red wooden pillars. The stone bases of the pillars are decorated with crude and bold carvings of strange animals such as magic lions and heavenly dragons. With a roof of yellow glazed tiles, the structure is distinguished by 6-layer brackets under two upturned eaves. The board above the east door is inscribed with four red characters "de mou tian di", which means that Kongzi's moral integrity is as unquestioned as the heaven and earth. The name of the west door—"dao guan gu jin" —means that Kongzi doctrines are unrivalled in history. All this demonstrates the esteemed role that Confucianism has played in creating traditional Chinese culture.

The Kuaidu Gate, the Yanggao Gate

The side doors of the second courtyard are called "kuai du men (gate)" and "yang gao men (gate)" respectively. People were allowed to enter Kong Temple via the front gate only on occasions of grand sacrificial rites. Otherwise, the Yanggao Gate was to be used.

The Yucui Gate, the Guande Gate

The side doors of the sixth courtyard outside the Dacheng Gate are named "yu cui men (gate)" and "guan de men (gate)". The two doors were first built in the Jin Dynasty. With a depth of two rooms and a width of three rooms, the doors are covered with yellow glazed tiles and upturned eaves. The name of the east door "yu cui" means "cultivating talented people of moral integrity and profound learning". The Chinese word "guan de" means "admiring Kongzi's virtues". As soon as you cross the Yucui Gate, you'll be in Kong Residence. This side door originally served as an everyday passage between Kong Residence and Kong Temple, open to passers-by. It is said that the Kong family once issued a prohibitive regulation that the passage of this door was open only to those in neat attire.

Witness of the Culture of Poetry and Rites

When you walk through the Tongwen Gate, you will be greeted by beautiful scenes teeming with the culture of poetry and rites. Let's tour the Kuiwen Pavilion and 13 Stele Pavilions first.

Kuiwen Tower —a Famous Depository Library in the East

Situated behind the Tongwen Gate, the Kuiwen Tower—a three-story imposing structure—is a depository library which is famous both at home and abroad for its rich collection of books as well as for its unique architecture. Immediately below the front eave there is a wooden inscription board on which the three characters "kui wen ge" (leading scholar tower) in the handwriting of Emperor Qianlong of the Qing Dynasty was surrounded by decorative dragon patterns. The Kuiwen Tower is the oldest building in

Kuiwen Tower

Kong Temple, a famous depository library in northern China during the Ming and Qing Dynasties and one of the ten most famous ancient towers in China.

The Kuiwen Tower was first built in 1018 (the 2nd year of the reign of Emperor Tianxi of the Northern Song Dynasty). Its original name "cang shu lou" (depository library) was replaced by "kui wen ge" when it was renovated in 1191 (the 2nd year of the reign of Emperor Mingchang of the Jin Dynasty). In the Chinese language, "kui" is considered as one of the 28 Chinese zodiacal constellations which are further divided into four groups. Of the western group of White Tiger, *kui* is listed as the first constellation. Composed of 16 stars, *kui* looks like a painting of Chinese characters. That's why the ancient people compared *kui* to the leading scholar. People looked upon Kongzi as the leading scholar in China and renamed the depository library of Kong Temple "kui wen ge".

Forest of Steles in the East

As it enjoys the special privilege of being a guardian of traditional Chinese culture, Qufu has collected several thousand steles of extreme cultural value. These ancient stone slabs together make up Qufu's forest of steles, one of the largest in China. Such a collection of tablets is rarely seen in the world, and it is renowned for its huge number, prolonged history and fine preservation. A great many valuable steles can be found in Kong Temple. The Imperial Tablets of the Ming Dynasty and Thirteen Stele Pavilions are among the most precious.

Imperial Tablets of the Ming Dynasty

In front of the Kuiwen Tower there are two stele pavilions. Two giant stone tablets outside the pavilions and two stone tablets inside are all imperial tablets of the Ming Dynasty. With a height of six metres and a width of two metres, the giant tablet is carved with round dragon designs at its top. The stone base is one metre high with a sculpture of *bixi* (a legendary giant turtle-like animal) supporting the heavy stone tablet. The handwritings

Bixi (Legendary Giant Turtle-like Animal)
Tradition has it that the dragon gave birth to nine sons. Every one of them possessed a special skill. His ninth son Bixi was good at bearing a heavy load. That's why he was entrusted with the job of carrying a stone tablet on his back.

The Chenghua Tablet to the East of the Tongwen Gate

of some inscriptions on the stone tablets are acknowledged models of calligraphy. Of the four imperial tablets, the one in the east pavilion is Emperor Zhu Yuanzhang's imperial instruction tablet established in 1371 (the 4th year of the reign of Emperor Hongwu). The one in front of the pavilion is the tablet commemorating the renovation of Kong Temple in 1418 (the 4th year of Emperor Chenghua). The one in the west pavilion is another commemoration of the renovation of Kong Temple undertaken during the period of Yongle under the reign of Emperor of Chengzu of the Ming Dynasty. The imperial tablet in front of the west pavilion marks the renovation of Kong Temple during the period of Hongzhi.

Throughout the Ming Dynasty, Kong Temple underwent several renovations. The three imperial tablets commemorating the renovations were established after its completion. The inscriptions on the tablets describe the purpose of the renovations: to hold Confucianism in esteem, expound the close relationship between Kongzi thought and Chinese society, and underscore the paramount importance of Kongzi thought in governing the state and ensuring national security.

Thirteen Stele Pavilions

The narrow courtyard behind the Kuiwen Tower is the sixth courtyard of Kong Temple. The courtyard is crowded with 13 pavilions of classical

A Bird's-Eye View of Thirteen Stele Pavilions

beauty. With eight on the south side and five on the north side, together these magnificent pavilions are called "Thirteen Pavilions for Sheltering Imperial Stone Tablets". All the 13 yellow-roofed and red-walled pavilions are of a square shape and decorated with octagonal eaves. The central two pavilions on the south side were built in the Yuan Dynasty. These two are flanked by two pavilions built in 1195 (the 6th year of the reign of Emperor Mingchang of the Jin Dynasty), which boast an unconventional and vigorous style of architecture. They are listed amongst the earliest structures of Kong Temple and among the most typical representations of ancient buildings in

Thirteen Stele Pavilions

China. All the other nine pavilions were built in the Qing Dynasty.

The existing 50 or so imperial stone tablets sheltered in the 13 pavilions were inscribed in the Chinese, Mongolian and Manchurian languages during the period of the Tang, Song, Jin, Yuan, Ming and Qing Dynasties and the Republic of China to record how the emperors of different dynasties conferred honorary titles posthumously to Kongzi and how sacrificial rites were held and how the temple was renovated.

Besides the courtyard of steles to the west of the front of the Kuiwen Tower, there are more stone tablets and stele pavilions in its front and back courtyards as well as in the walls. The pavilions were built especially to shelter the imperial stone tablets, hence the name of "Imperial Stele Pavilion". In addition to the 13 stele pavilions, there are two more on both sides of the entrance of the Kuiwen Tower.

Hongwu Stele Pavilion

There are many more small stone tablets standing in the open air to form the "small forest of steles". These tablets are inscribed with the experiences of various emperors in renovating the temple, paying homage to Kongzi and offering sacrifices in the temple. These are very precious historical recordings.

According to statistics, there are over 1,000 stone tablets in Kong Temple, including those specially established to offer sacrifices to Kongzi, show homage to Kongzi, record the renovation of Kong Temple and commend Kongzi's virtues and merits. In terms of numbers and time span, the forest of steles in Kong Temple can be considered as a treasure house for the study of Chinese history and culture. With a great variety of different styles of handwriting, the forest of steles can be regarded as a museum of Chinese calligraphy.

Emperor Kangxi Giant Tablet

A Comprehensive Collection of Oriental Culture

When you pass by the 13 stele pavilions, you'll see five gates standing side by side in front of you. The central one is "da cheng men" (Dacheng Gate) while the two on its east and west sides are "jin sheng men" (Jinsheng Gate) and "yu zhen men" (Yuzhen Gate) respectively. Passing through any of these three gates, will lead you to three different paths. When you enter the Dacheng Gate, you'll be greeted by a series of main buildings of Kong Temple: the Dacheng Hall, East Wing and West Wing, the Apricot Platform, the Chamber Hall and the Shengji Hall. Modelled after the structure of an imperial palace, the yellow-tiled and red-walled buildings look imposing and solemn. This is the main venue for holding sacrificial rites.

The Footsteps of a Sage —Growing Trees and Cultivating Talents

As an old Chinese saying goes, "It takes ten years to grow trees, but a hundred to cultivate people." By drawing an analogy between tree growing and talent cultivation, the Chinese saying implies that the cultivation of talents is an arduous and prolonged undertaking. It is a happy coincidence that what attracts you most in the main buildings of Kong Temple is none

Left: The Chinese Juniper Planted by the Late Teacher

other than the Chinese juniper tree planted by Kongzi himself and the Apricot Platform where Kongzi gave lectures.

Sacred Tree—the Chinese Juniper Planted by the Late Teacher

Behind the Dacheng Gate, the Chinese juniper tree is located on the east side. This 16-metre-high tree is so large that one can just get one's arms around its trunk. The tall crown of the verdant tree spreads a canopy of green leaves overhead. Despite its size, most people will be so attracted by the magnificent Dacheng Hall when they cross the Dacheng Gate that they pay no heed to this tree. Tradition has it that this Chinese juniper was planted by Kongzi himself. It is now protected by a stone fence and a stone tablet nearby is inscribed with the words: "the Chinese juniper planted by the late teacher".

Sacred Platform to Spread Culture—the Apricot Platform

Opposite to the Chinese juniper tree planted by Kongzi himself is a grove of apricot trees surrounding a square pavilion. Enveloped by a stone balustrade, the pavilion attractively sets off the Dacheng Hall. This is the Apricot Platform, which men of letters have spoken highly of throughout Chinese history. Decorated with coloured drawings, the yellow-roofed and red-pillared pavilion looks splendid and magnificent. There is a stone incense burner with exquisite carvings. In early spring, the apricot trees surrounding the forum are clad in fragrant blossom.

The Stone Tablet in the Apricot Platform Pavilion

Apricot Platform

Emperor Qianlong was inspired to write a poem on seeing this beautiful sight during his second visit to Qufu.

It is said the Apricot Platform is the place where Kongzi gave lectures. In 1018 (the 2nd year of the reign of Emperor Tianxi of the Northern Song Dynasty), Kong Daofu, Kongzi's descendant of the 45th generation, was in charge of supervising the renovation of Kong Temple. He had the main hall moved backward and expanded. The old site of the main hall was replaced by a platform. With the apricot trees planted around the platform, this place was named the Apricot Platform. A pavilion was built on the platform in the Jin Dynasty and the famous scholar Dang Huaiying wrote the two characters "xing tan" (apricot platform) in the seal style of calligraphy. In modern Chinese, the word "xing tan" is used to denote a "lecture room" or "field of education".

The Dacheng Hall
—Sacred Hall in the East

Dacheng Gate

The Dacheng Gate—the seventh gate of Kong Temple—lies at the back of the Thirteen Stele Pavilions. With pillars and steps carved with dragon patterns, the yellow-tiled building with upturned eaves looks splendid and imposing. In the early period of the Song Dynasty, the gate was called "yi men (gate)" and served as the main entrance of Kong Temple. It was rebuilt and then renovated in the Ming and Qing Dynasties respectively. The horizontal board is inscribed with the three characters "da cheng men" written by Emperor Yongzheng of the Qing Dynasty. This gate was open only when sacrificial rites were held. People otherwise used the Jinsheng Gate and the Yuzhen Gate.

Kongzi showed respect to sacred lords in history and carried forward the brilliant culture of ancient China. Mengzi said that Kongzi had epitomized the thoughts of previous sages and wise men. People of later generations accepted Mengzi's view. It is for this reason that both the gate and hall were named "da cheng" (great thoughts of previous sages and wise men) when they were renovated in the Song Dynasty.

As soon as you step through the Dacheng Gate, you will see the Apricot Platform. You'll then be immediately attracted by an imposing building standing on a high platform beyond the Apricot Platform. The eye-catching characters denoting the name of the building—Dacheng Hall—can be seen in the distance. The Dacheng Hall is the principal structure of Kong Temple.

Dacheng Gate

The Dacheng Hall

The Dacheng Hall, originally named the Wenxuanwang Hall and the Xuansheng Hall in succession, was first built in 1018 (the 2nd year of the reign of Emperor Tianxi of the Song Dynasty). Emperor Huizong of the Song Dynasty issued an imperial edict to change the name of the hall and wrote "da cheng dian (hall)" himself on the inscription board. Later, the Dacheng Hall was struck by lightning and burned to the ground. The hall was rebuilt several times. When it was renovated in 1724, Emperor Yongzheng of the Qing Dynasty wrote a new inscription board. The imperial government of the Qing Dynasty gave special permission to design and rebuild the Dacheng Hall according to the standard of an imperial palace and sent some experienced palace craftsmen to work on the site.

Dacheng Hall

The Dacheng Hall of Kong Temple in Qufu is the main venue used to hold sacrificial rites in memory of Kongzi. Known as the soul of Kong Temple, the Dacheng Hall and other two famous halls in China—the Taihe Hall in the Palace Museum of Beijing and the Tiankuang Hall in the Dai Temple of Tai'an—are called "the three magnificent halls in the east".

Dragon Pillars and Horizontal Inscription Board

The most distinctive features of the Dacheng Hall are the numerous dragon pillars and examples of handwriting from ancient emperors. The Dacheng Hall is surrounded by 28 stone pillars all intricately carved with dragon patterns. The carvings were done on complete pieces of marble by

Statute of Kongzi and Inscription Boards in Dacheng Hall

Horizontal Inscription Board of Dacheng Hall

the craftsmen of Huizhou sent by the imperial government in 1500 (the 13th year of the reign of Emperor Hongzhi of the Ming Dynasty). The 10 pillars in front of the hall are especially spectacular with two dragons of different shapes and expressions carved on each pillar. The other 18 pillars are each carved with 9 dragons around them. The meticulous craftsmen carved a total of 1296 dragons on the pillars. It is said that as these decorations of dragon carvings surpassed even those of the imperial palace. When emperor Qianlong came to offer sacrifices to Kongzi, the pillars were wrapped up in yellow satins under the pretence of putting up decorations to welcome the emperor. In actual fact, the pillars were covered out of fear of reproach from the emperor on account of the pillars intricate splendour.

Dragon-Carved Stone Pillars in Dacheng Hall

On both the outside and the inside of the Dacheng Hall are 10 inscription boards and three antithetical couplets written by emperors themselves. This rare occurrence has made the Dacheng Hall the most precious of all the ancient buildings in China.

When you enter the Dacheng Hall, you will stand face-to-face with a 3.35-metre-high statue of Kongzi sitting in a huge shrine decorated with carved dragons and golden patterns. In front of the statue there is an exquisitely carved memorial tablet with the following golden words on a red background written in the middle:

Sacrificial Vessels and Musical Instruments Displayed in Dacheng Hall

"memorial tablet for Kongzi, the greatest sage and the deceased teacher". The statue of Kongzi is dressed like an emperor. His full forehead and slightly narrowed face show the superhuman wisdom of a sage.

Four minor sages and 12 wise men

The statue of Kongzi is accompanied on both sides by the statues of four minor sages and 12 wise men. Of the four minor sages highly esteemed by the people of later generations, Yan Hui and Zisi are on the east side while Zengzi and Mengzi are on the west side. Of the 12 wise men, Min Ziqian, Zhong Gong, Zigong, Zilu, Zixia and You Ruo are on the east side and Ran Boniu, Zai Wo, Ran You, Ziyou, Zizhang and Zhu Xi are on the west side. Zhu Xi was looked upon as the Kongzi of the Song Dynasty. The other 11 wise men were all Kongzi's disciples.

According to *The Analects of Confucius*, in the four classes Kongzi taught, the following 10 were ranked as most brilliant students: "Yan Yuan, Min Ziqian, Ran Boniu and Zhong Gong (in respect of virtues); Zai Wo and Zigong (in respect of language); Ran You and Ji Lu (in respect of politics); Ziyou and Zixia (in respect of literature)." People of later generations called them "10 wise men". When Yan Hui (also called Yan Yuan) was promoted to the status of "minor sage", Zengzi became one of the 10 wise men. After Zengzi was promoted to the rank of "minor sage", Zizhang became of the 10 wise men. During the reign of Emperor Kangxi of the Qing Dynasty Zhu Xi was promoted to the rank of "wise man". During the reign of Emperor Qianlong You Ruo was promoted to the rank of wise man. Ever since then, 12 wise men were generally acknowledged in China.

In front of every statue there is an altar table, an incense altar and sacrificial vessels. Displayed in the hall are a complete set of musical instruments used for sacrificial rites in memory of Kongzi.

Zhu Xi
Zhu Xi, also called Yuanhui, Zhonghui, Hui'an, Kaoting and Ziyang, was a philosopher and educator of the Southern Song Dynasty. When he was young, he read extensively and knew how to digest the different schools of thought. He inherited and developed the idealist doctrines advocated by Cheng Hao and Cheng Yi. He founded his own idealist philosophy. The doctrines proposed by two Cheng's and himself were known as the Cheng-Zhu School of Thought. He devoted more than 50 years of his life to education. The idealist philosophy initiated by him was adopted by the ruling class of the feudal society in its later periods as a theoretical tool and was upgraded to the status of authentic Confucianism during the Ming and Qing Dynasties.

Outdoor Scene of East Wing of Dacheng Hall

Two Wings
—the Final Settling Place of Great Thinkers of Confucianism in Chinese History

People come to Kong Temple to pay homage not only to Kongzi, the four minor sages and 12 wise men, but also to the great thinkers of Confucianism through Chinese history that are enshrined in the two complexes of rooms.

On both sides of the front courtyard of the Dacheng Hall there are wings with 40 rooms each. These green-tiled and red-pillared rooms connected by long corridors are called "two wings" where people of later generations enshrined and worshipped the great thinkers of Confucianism in history. Some alterations were made in every dynasty as to the list of

Indoor Scene of East Wing of Dacheng Hall

qualified Confucian scholars. In addition to the disciples of Kongzi, the qualified Confucian scholars include the great thinkers of later generations who tirelessly spread Confucianism in the different periods of Chinese history, such as Dong Zhongshu, Han Yu, Cheng Hao, Wang Yangming and Gu Yanwu. They respected Kongzi as the leading scholar and role model of his time, looked upon six Confucian classical works as guidance and were proud of carrying forward the Confucian orthodoxy. They further developed Kongzi thought, popularized Confucianism among the Chinese people and spread Kongzi doctrines to every corner of Chinese society. The number of Confucian scholars that qualified for being enshrined in the two complexes was increased from around 20 in the Tang Dynasty to 156 in the Republic of China. The original portraits of those Confucian scholars were replaced by statues in the Jin Dynasty, which were further replaced by wooden memorial tablets enshrined in every independent shrine. As a result, Kong Temple became the symbol of showing respect to Kongzi and worshiping Confucianism, and a sacred place frequented by scholars of different times.

Displayed in the northern parts of the two wings are some 584 stone inscriptions. The Yuhonglou's collection of stone inscriptions are the work of Kong Jisu—Kongzi's descendant—who did the carving modelled on original calligraphic works of famous calligraphers in Chinese history.

Mrs. Kong's Chamber Hall

Walking backward along the winding corridor of the Dacheng Hall, you'll see another splendid hall—a memorial hall where people offer sacrifices to Kongzi's wife, also called Madame Bing, nee Guan. Mrs. Kong's Chamber Hall is as famous as the Kuiwen Tower and the Dacheng Hall.

With a width of seven rooms, a depth of four rooms and a height of 20 metres, the Chamber Hall is decorated with golden foil dragons on the crossbeams and phoenixes on the coffers. On the 22 eight-facet waterstone-polished stone pillars in the winding corridor are carved patterns of phoenixes playing amidst peonies. All the designs are accurate replicas of the empress's chamber in an imperial palace. In the Chamber

Chamber Hall

Eight-facet Water Stone-Polished Stone Pillars in Front of the Chamber Hall

Hall, there is a shrine carved with dragons and phoenixes with a wooden memorial tablet inscribed with the following words: "memorial tablet for the wife of Kongzi, the greatest sage and the deceased teacher".

Mrs. Bing, nee Guan—Kongzi's wife—was born in the Song Kingdom. She married Kongzi at the age of 19. She gave birth to a son and a daughter. She died seven years before Kongzi. There are no accounts of her life in historical records. However, in traditional Chinese society a woman usually basked in the glory of her husband. After the death of Kongzi, people paid homage to her as well as to Kongzi. A chamber hall was built in the Tang Dynasty for people to offer sacrifices to her. In the early days there was a statue in the hall. However, when the chamber hall was rebuilt after being damaged by fire, a memorial tablet was erected in its place. In the Song Dynasty, the system of presenting famous personages with posthumous titles was adopted. With the elevated position of Kongzi in society, she was honoured in succession with the titles of "Lady of Yun Kingdom", "Lady of Sage Prince of Wenxuan" and "Lady of the Greatest Sage and Teacher".

"Model Teacher for All Ages" in the Handwriting of Emperor Kangxi

The Shengji Hall
—Display of Kongzi's Sacred Life

Behind the Chamber Hall is the last courtyard of Kong Temple. The hall standing there is called the Shengji Hall (the Sage's Life Hall). The five-room hall was built in 1592 (the 20th year of the reign of Emperor Wanli of the Ming Dynasty) under the supervision of He Chuguang, the Imperial Roving Commissioner, to store the Paintings of the Sage's Life, a set of paintings depicting the life of Kongzi.

The Paintings of the Sage's Life are composed of eight pieces of introductory writings and 112 paintings with illustrations, depicting the whole life and teachings of Kongzi. It starts with the story of his birth after

Outdoor Scene of the Shengji Hall

his mother prayed at Mount Nishan, and ends with the story about his disciples keeping vigil beside his grave. Two paintings describe how Liu Bang, the Emperor Gaozu of the Han Dynasty, and Zhao Heng, the Emperor of Zhenzong of the Song Dynasty, offered sacrifices to Kongzi. As the first sequence of pictures to depict a story in China, this set of paintings was of great historical and artistic value.

The eye-catching four Chinese characters "wan shi shi biao" (the model teacher for all ages) carved on a stone were written by Emperor Kangxi himself. The six classic works Kongzi had edited and revised became essential reading for the scholars of later generations. The classic Confucian works were compulsory reading materials for those attending imperial civil examinations. As a result, students of Chinese history mainly followed the teachings of Kongzi and Confucianism. The scholars looked upon Kongzi as the founder of the Confucian school and felt proud of being his followers. In 1684 (the 23rd year of the reign of Emperor Kangxi), Emperor Kangxi came to Qufu to pay homage to Kongzi and wrote "the model teacher for all ages" on a horizontal inscription board, which was hung in the Dacheng Hall. Later,

"Model Teacher for All Ages" in the Handwriting of Emperor Kangxi

the four characters were carved on a stone and the tablet was put in the Shengji Hall. In schools throughout China, either the portrait of Kongzi or his memorial tablet was set up with the four characters "wan shi shi biao" (the model teacher for all ages) written on it. Whenever a student went to school, he or she was first required to pay homage to Kongzi.

On display in the Shengji Hall are the famous portraits of Kongzi, painted by the two of the most well-known painters in China—Gu Kaizhi of the Eastern Jin Dynasty and Wu Daozi of the Tang Dynasty. These portraits are Kongzi leaning on the desk, Kongzi holding a post of Minister of Justice of the Lu Kingdom and Kongzi accompanied by Yanzi. On the west side, there is an exhibit of the famous calligraphic work "Ode to Kongzi" written by Mi Fu, a great calligrapher of the Song Dynasty, in which he eulogized Kongzi as a sage not to be found either in the past or in the future. There are several imperial stone tablets written by Emperor Kangxi and Emperor Qianlong. All the exhibits in the Shengji Hall are the works produced by people of later generations to show respect to Kongzi.

Respect for Ancestors and the Culture of Rites and Music

The Chengsheng Gate and the Qisheng Gate on either side of the Dacheng Gate lead to the east path and the west path respectively. The east path is where people offer sacrifices to Kongzi's ancestors of five generations, while the west path is for offering sacrifices to Kongzi's parents. This practice reflects the tradition of holding one's ancestors in high esteem.

The east path of Kong Temple lies is the place where Kongzi originally lived. The places of historic interest along this path include the Poetry and Rites Hall, the ancient well and the Lu Wall towards the front of the temple and the Chongsheng Ancestral Hall and Family Temple towards the back. These buildings serve to embody the Confucian culture of poetry, ancient texts, rites and music. The descendants of Kongzi offered sacrifices to their ancestors here.

Essence of the Confucian Culture of Poetry and Rites

When you enter the Chengsheng Gate, you'll see five rooms in the first courtyard. It is said that Kongzi used to live there. There is a story in

Poetry and Rites Hall

The Analects of Confucius: One day, Kong Li passed by Kongzi, who was standing in the courtyard. Kongzi asked his son whether he had studied *The Book of Songs* and Kong Li said "no". Kongzi said, "You won't know how to talk if you don't study *The Book of Songs*." Kong Li thus began to study *The Book of Songs*. Another time, Kongzi asked him whether he had studied *The Rites*, and Kong Li again replied, "no". Kongzi then said, "You won't know how to get along with the world or conduct yourself in society if you don't study *The Rites*." And so Kong Li began to study *The Rites*. Kongzi's assignation of the utmost importance to these two cultural documents is the reason why the Poetry and Rites Hall was set up there by people of later generations.

Ancient Well of Kongzi's Abode

Ancient Well of Kongzi's Abode

Turning past the Poetry and Rites Hall, you'll step into a deep and quiet courtyard, where you will feel serene and secluded from the world. There is an ancient well with a stone tablet nearby inscribed with "the well of Kongzi's abode".

Located on the east path, Kongzi's abode is also called "Queli Residence". Outside the Yucui Gate of Kong Temple, there is an inconspicuous small door with an inscription board hung at the top. "The door of Kongzi's abode" indicates the oldest and most meaningful place in Kong Temple—the place where Kongzi once lived.

Tradition has it that Kongzi and his family lived on the water drawn from this ancient well. The clear water in the three-metre-deep well was regarded as sacred water. Emperor Qianlong pronounced his intention to acknowledge Kongzi as his teacher by drinking a scoop of the well water. Originally, in order to commemorate this anecdote, people built a pavilion to shelter a stone tablet inscribed with "Ode to the Well of Kongzi's Abode" written by Emperor Qianlong himself. There are engraved characters on the four sides of the tablet. During his eight visits to Qufu, Emperor Qianlong wrote short remarks five times to express his respect to the Confucian culture.

Lu Wall

By the side of the well, stands a high screen wall facing the gate with a stone tablet inscribed in red with the two characters "lu bi" (Lu Wall). This inconspicuous wall held a very important position in the minds of Chinese scholars, because historical documents of great significance were discovered here. Some people called this wall "the windbreak for classic Confucian culture".

According to *History of Han*, when the First Emperor of the Qin Dynasty initiated a campaign to burn books and bury Confucian scholars alive, Kong Fu, Kongzi's descendant of the ninth generation, built a wall and hid the classic works within it. During the reign of Emperor Jing of the Western Han Dynasty, Liu Yu, the King Gong of the Lu Kingdom, happened to find in the wall such classic works as *Collection of Ancient Texts*, *The Book of Etiquette and Ceremonial*, *The Analects of Confucius* and *The Book of Filial Piety* when he dismantled Kongzi's house to make way for the expansion of his palace. These classic works were written in tadpole characters and were called either "classics in ancient script" or "classics from the Kong wall". At that time, the classic works were written in the official script. To the people of the Western Han Dynasty, the script of the classical works discovered in the Lu Wall was entirely different from their own modern script.

If it was only a matter of their script being different, nobody should have been so excited over them. But this batch of classic works was of great significance to the Han Dynasty for a plethora of reasons. After all, a huge amount of Confucian works had been burnt by the First Emperor of the Qin Dynasty, and the ruling class now intended to revive Confucianism, but were lacking in classic Confucian works. Following the discovery in the wall, the emperor of the Han Dynasty issued an edict to hunt for more of these ancient works. They went to the aged Confucian scholars for help and asked them to write in the official script the classics they could recite. These were called "Confucian classics in modern script". The doctorate of classics

Burn Books and Bury Confucian Scholars Alive
In 213 BC (the 34th year of the reign of the First Emperor of the Qin Dynasty) the Prime Minister, Li Si, believed the Legalist School of Thought was the only legitimate theory and proposed that all the books of other schools of thought be burned. The following year the First Emperor of the Qin Dynasty was furious that the alchemists failed to find the elixir of life for him and buried 460 alchemists alive in Xianyang. This incident inflicted a severe blow upon Confucianism and the Confucian School of Thought.

Lu Wall

set up in the Han Dynasty required the candidates to study Confucian classics in modern script. Those doctors good at Confucian classics attained a prominent position in the spheres of learning and politics. However, the Confucian classics discovered in the Lu Wall were different from those used by the Confucian scholars in the early period of the Han Dynasty. So far as *A Collection of Ancient Texts* is concerned, the ancient-script copy was different from the modern-script copy in the number of texts and in the wording of some texts. For this reason, the majority of Confucian scholars of the Han Dynasty rejected the ancient-script copy. However, some scholars did bestow great praise upon the ancient-script copies and thus founded the ancient-script school of Confucian classics. A heated debate between the advocates of the two different schools of thought was started, and this debate became one of the notable landmarks in China's academic history.

In order to commemorate this historical event, the people of the Jin Dynasty built halls inside Kongzi's abode. When Kong Temple was renovated in 1500 (the 13th year of the reign of Emperor Hongzhi of the Ming Dynasty), the Jinsi Hall was moved to the west path of Kong Temple. The Poetry and Rites Hall was established in Kongzi's abode. Later, the Lu Wall was erected to commend Kong Fu for his contributions to the protection of cultural classics.

Be Always Grateful to Ancestors

The Chongsheng Ancestral Hall

To the north of the Poetry and Rites Hall and behind the Lu Wall, a path leading backwards is flanked by two stone tablets inscribed with the names of Kongzi's offspring of lineal descent, which is regarded as an important record for the study of the history of Kong family.

Shrine for Genealogy Tablet in Kong Temple

The five-room hall standing on a terrace at the end of the path is the Chongsheng Ancestral Hall. Of the eight stone pillars carved with patterns, the middle two are carved with two dragons playing with a pearl. Not as imposing as the dragon pillars of the Dacheng Hall, these pillars can still be regarded as examples of exquisite craftsmanship. Kongzi's ancestors of the

Chongsheng Ancestral Hall

previous five generations are enshrined in the ancestral hall. Also worshipped in this hall are the fathers of the four minor sages—Yan Hui, Zengzi, Zisi and Mengzi and the fathers of the great Confucian scholars of the Song Dynasty—Zhou Dunyi, Zhang Zai, Cheng Hao, Cheng Yi, Zhu Xi and Cai Chen.

Family Temple

The seven-room courtyard behind the Chongsheng Ancestral Hall is Kongzi's family temple where the descendants of Kongzi offered sacrifices to their ancestors. Confucianism attaches a great importance to the family. In traditional feudal society, people had a strong sense of family ties and responsibilities, and those of higher social status usually had their own family temple. Kong Family Temple along the east path of Kong Temple is a typical representative of this tradition. Enshrined in the family temple are

Gate of the Family Temple in Kong Temple

Kongzi and his wife in the centre; his son, Kong Li, and his wife on his left; his grandson, Kong Ji, and his wife on his right; as well as his descendant of the 43rd generation, Kong Renyu and his wife.

The Temple of the Village God

Standing behind the family temple is the Temple of the Village God. Kongzi was born at Mount Nishan in the southeast of Qufu. You can find Nishan Reservoir—the biggest reservoir in Qufu today—in this beautiful area of green mountains and crystal-clear waters. Tradition has it that the birth of Kongzi was thanks to the sacred spirit of Nishan. People of later generations conferred the title of Marquis of Yusheng to the God of Nishan. The original temple was the place where people worshipped the Marquis of Yusheng. When the Marquis of Yusheng was moved to the Kong

Sacred Kitchen

temple of Nishan, this place was turned into the Temple to pay homage to the Village God.

Sacred Kitchen

Behind the Temple of the Village God there is an independent courtyard surrounded by five frontal rooms and four side rooms on both sides. This courtyard served as the kitchen, where sacrifices were prepared for sacrificial rites. According to Mengzi, whenever people were to see living birds and animals, a virtuous man would be reluctant to see them die; whenever people were to see them wail sadly, a virtuous man would be reluctant to eat their meat. That's why a virtuous man put his kitchen in a faraway place—the kitchen of Kong Temple is far enough away from the Dacheng Hall that no sad wails of animals could be heard.

Front Hall of Kong Temple Looked at from the Door of the Sacred Kitchen

Pay a Debt of Gratitude to His Parents

To the west of the Dacheng Gate, the Qisheng Gate leads to the west path of Kong Temple, a place where people offer sacrifices to Kongzi's parents. You'll find the following historical relics along the west path: the Jinsi Hall, the Prince of Qisheng Hall, the Chamber Hall of Prince of Qisheng.

The Jinsi Hall

When you pass the Qisheng Gate, you'll see five green-tiled rooms on a terrace. This is called the Jinsi Hall. It was built for the purpose of commemorating Kong Fu for his hiding of Confucian classics in the Lu Wall. When you enter the Jinsi Hall, you'll see in front of you a horizontal board written by Emperor Qianlong. On display in the hall is a stone carved with the four characters "yu tian di can" written by Emperor Qianlong for the Dacheng Hall, which means "Kongzi thought and doctrines are as enduring as heaven and earth". The west side room is the storeroom of the musical instruments bestowed by Emperor Kangxi on Kong Temple. The musical instruments were used at sacrificial rites.

The Prince of Qisheng Hall

There are three parallel gates behind the Jinsi Hall. The main gate leads to a magnificent hall. This is the Prince of Qisheng Hall where people offered sacrifices to Kongzi's father, Kong Shuliang or Kong He.

In line with the traditions of feudal society, Kongzi's elevated status meant his parents were also honoured with noble titles. In 1330, the titles of "Prince of Qisheng" and "Lady of Qisheng" were conferred on Kongzi's father and mother respectively.

The five-room hall standing on a terrace is covered with a green-tile roof. Of the pattern-carved stone pillars, the middle two are carved with the pattern of two dragons playing with a pearl. The original hall was built in the Song Dynasty. What you see now was rebuilt after a fire in the second year of the reign of Emperor Yongzheng.

Kongzi's ancestors were noblemen of the Song Kingdom. However, due to social upheaval and transformation, they were forced to leave their homeland and travelled to the Lu Kingdom. The Kong family belonged to the declining stratum of the noble class when Kongzi's father became the head of the family. Kong Shuliang was reduced to the rank of warrior.

Chamber Hall of Prince of Qisheng

Behind the Prince of Qisheng Hall is a three-room chamber hall sharing the same terrace with the former. This is where people offered sacrifices to Kongzi's mother, Yan Zhengzai.

Stone and Brick Carvings in the Sacred Kitchen

Kong Residence
—the No.1 Residence in the East

With the scope of construction as large as that of an imperial palace, the private residence of the Kong family has remained for thousands of years a unique phenomenon in Chinese history. The architecture, decoration and layout of Kong Residence will help us better understand the Chinese people's strong sense of family and savour traditional Chinese culture.

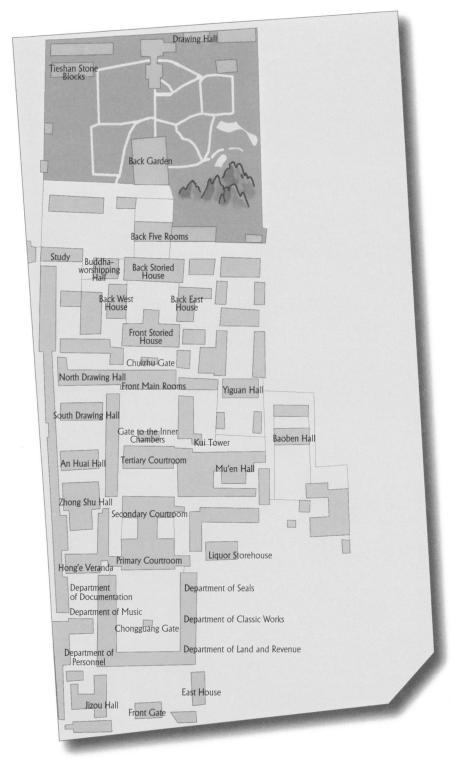

A Map of Kong Residence

While Kong Temple is the embodiment of great Kongzi thought, Kong Residence is a reflection of the eminent position of his offspring.

Kong Residence, originally called "the Duke of Yansheng Residence", is situated to the east of Kong Temple in Qufu. This was the living place of Kongzi's offspring of lineal descent. The title of the "Duke of Yansheng" was conferred on Kong Zongyuan, Kongzi's descendent of the 46th generation, by Emperor Renzong in 1055 (the 2nd year of the reign of Zhihe of the Nothern Song Dynasty). The title was passed on from generation to generation and lasted for 32 generations living in the Song, Yuan, Ming and Qing Dynasties. With the scope of construction as large as that of an imperial palace, the private residence of Kong family has remained for thousands of years a unique phenomenon in Chinese history. The architecture, decoration and layout of Kong Residence will help us better understand the Chinese people's strong sense of family and savour traditional Chinese culture.

Eminent Position of the Kong Family

Kongzi enjoyed the same status as emperors and kings while his offspring offered sacrifices to him in Kong Temple. The Kong family has lasted for over 2000 years with a well-recorded family tree and the perfect order of seniority. This kind of situation is rarely seen in world history.

Historical Development
of Kong Residence

After the death of Kongzi, his offspring lived to the east of Kong Temple. They looked after the relics left behind by Kongzi, offered sacrifices to Kongzi, studied and spread Kongzhi thought. The inherited residence of the Kong family was passed on from generation to generation. The scope of the residence did not change much before the Northern Song Dynasty. By the end of the Northern Song Dynasty, it was composed of only a couple of dozen rooms.

During the Ming and Qing Dynasties, the central government granted great power and wealth to the Kong family. As a result, Kong Residence was gradually expanded. Zhu Yuanzhang, the first emperor of the Ming Dynasty, promoted the Duke of Yansheng to the rank of grade-one official and bestowed a lot of land and tenant peasants upon him. The Kong family had to take charge of its financial, domestic and clan affairs as well as the administrative affairs of Qufu. Only a large administrative organ was capable of taking on these multiple duties.

In the early period of the Ming Dynasty, the Duke of Yansheng Residence was built with the appropriations of the central government. It was renovated several times and was expanded to its present-day size. Li Dongyang and Yan Song—two high-ranking officials of the central government—played an important role as the supervisors of the

Yansheng
In Chinese "yan" means "flowing water" and "continuing". The word "yansheng" means "to continue and develop Confucian doctrines".

Gate of Kongzi's Abode

construction. Both of them became in-laws of the Duke of Yansheng when Li betrothed his daughter and Yan betrothed his granddaughter to him.

Kong Residence, built predominantly in the Ming and Qing Dynasties, covers an area of 240 *mu* (1 *mu*= 0.067 hectare) with 463 halls and rooms. With a layout of three paths and a depth of nine courtyards, Kong Residence enjoyed the highest architectural specifications in ancient China, thus demonstrating the great regard for and high status of Kongzi.

Emperors of Various Dynasties Show Respect to the Kong Family

While conferring posthumously one honorary title after another on Kongzi, the feudal rulers in China also granted official positions and special privileges to his descendants. In Chinese history no other family has ever enjoyed as many imperial benefits of wealth and power as the Kong family.

Starting from the Western Han Dynasty, the Kong family received many imperial favours and promotions.

Before the Song Dynasty, Kongzi's offspring usually enjoyed the status of marquis. There was only one exception when Emperor Xuanzong of the Tang Dynasty conferred the title of Duke of Wenxuan on them. Emperor Renzong of the Northern Song Dynasty conferred the title of the Duke of Yansheng on Kong Zongyuan, Kongzi's descendant of the 46th generation. The word "yansheng" in Chinese means that the male offspring of Kongzi will procreate from generation to generation and Kongzi thought will be carried forward forever. The title of the Duke of Yansheng lasted for 880 years over 32 generations until Kong Decheng, Kongzi's descendant of the 77th generation.

In Chinese history, political upheavals resulted in the division of the Duke of Yansheng. Since the Southern Song Dynasty, the offspring of lineal descent were divided into two branches—the southern clan and the northern clan. Being loyal to two different dynasties, two Dukes of Yansheng in the south and north of China respectively co-existed at the same time. The Jin Dynasty in the north of China sent an army southward and occupied Qufu. The then Duke of Yansheng, Kong Duanyou, Kongzi's descendant of the 48th generation, and some of his clansmen followed Emperor Gaozong and moved to Zhejiang. They lived there for generations and were called the southern branch of the Kong clan. In order to cultivate a sense of identity among the Han people who commanded a majority of the population, the rulers of the Jin Dynasty showed respect to their traditional ideology and culture. They held in esteem Kongzi and his descendants who remained in

Rank of Nobility
In ancient China the nobility were divided into five ranks: duke, marquis, earl, viscount and baron.

Qufu by conferring the title of the Duke of Yansheng on Kong Yuancuo, Kongzi's descendant of the 50th generation, hence the coexistence of two simultaneous Dukes of Yansheng in Chinese history. When the Yuan Dynasty established by Mongolians unified the whole country, the Duke of Yansheng in the south offered to concede his title to the northern branch of the Kong clan in Qufu to express his gratitude to Kongzi's offspring there for their protection and safeguarding of their forefathers' temple, residence and forest. In order to commend the modesty on the part of the southern branch, the government of the Yuan Dynasty conferred the title of "Doctor of the Imperial Academy in Five Confucian Classics" on Kongzi's descendants of the southern branch. The title of the Duke of Yansheng was inherited by Kongzi's offspring of the northern branch, thus putting an end to the coexistence of two Dukes of Yansheng in China.

Before the Song Dynasty, Kongzi's descendants did not hold any positions as high-ranking officials. Most of them served as the county magistrate of Qufu. Only the Duke of Yansheng, Kong Duanyou, held a position as the magistrate of Chenzhou Prefecture. However, during the Ming and Qing Dynasties, the political status of the Duke of Yansheng was greatly promoted to a Grade-one Official. In the Qing Dynasty, the Duke of Yansheng was further promoted to the highest rank of civil officials. In spite of this promotion in rank, the Duke of Yansheng continued to fulfil his special obligations to study hard and cultivate himself, act as a role model for officials, the populace and intellectuals, hold sacrificial rites in memory of Kongzi, manage the affairs of the Kong clan and administer the county of Qufu. In the Qing Dynasty, the Duke of Yansheng

The Tripod Presented to Kong Residence by Emperor Qianlong

no longer took on the concurrent position as county magistrate of Qufu. But he maintained the right to recommend the candidate for the post by standing as guarantor.

The Duke of Yansheng was often appointed by the emperor to serve as the teacher of the prince and interpreter of Confucian classics for the emperor and high-ranking officials. The governments of various dynasties bestowed to the Kong family a large amount of land, forest, peasants, valuable relics and curios. As a result, the houses where Kongzi's offspring lived became sumptuous and impressive. As the Duke of Yansheng was often required to go to the capital on business, the emperor bestowed to him a mansion house in Beijing in 1646 (the third year of the reign of Emperor Shunzhi of the Qing Dynasty).

The Biggest Aristocrat in China

The Duke of Yansheng was a great aristocrat who enjoyed special privileges in feudal China. The rank of Duke of Yansheng was upgraded in succession from a grade-eight official in the Song Dynasty, to grade three in the Yuan Dynasty, grade one in the Ming Dynasty, to the top of all civil officials in the Qing Dynasty. He was granted by the emperor of the Qing Dynasty the special right to ride a horse in the Forbidden City in Beijing and walk along an imperial path.

With the passage of over 2000 years, Kongzi's offspring have lived in various places of the world. A multitude of his descendants have their own branches of the family tree. Still, Qufu is inhabited by the biggest branch of the Kong clan. According to recent statistics, more than 200,000 of the Kong clan live in Qufu. In every village of Qufu, you will find Kongzi's descendants.

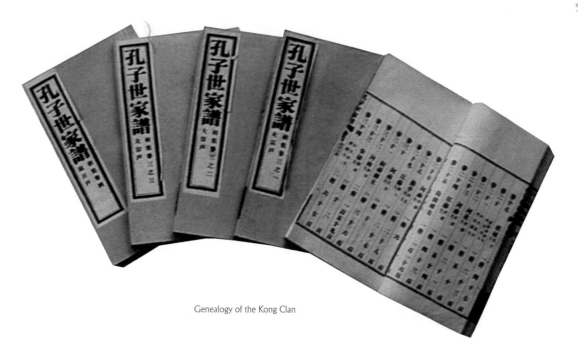

Genealogy of the Kong Clan

Kongzi's offspring of lineal descent lived primarily in Kong Residence. Before the Tang Dynasty, only Kongzi's eldest son and his descendants lived in Queli residence. In later periods, especially after the Song Dynasty, the multiplication of people of lineal descent made it impossible for them to live together in the original abode. The younger brother of the Duke of Yansheng had to build a house elsewhere. As a result, in addition to the Residence for the Duke of Yansheng, there are several mansion houses for the people of the Kong family in Qufu.

Prior to the Ming Dynasty, no specific name was assigned to Kongzi's descendant according to his position in the family hierarchy. Zhu Yuanzhang, the Empror of Taizu of the Ming Dynasty granted the naming system to the Kong family. Ever since then, every family member was named according to his seniority in the Kong clan. During the reign of Emperor Chongzhen of

Documentation of Kong Residence

the Ming Dynasty and the reign of Emperor Tongzhi of the Qing Dynasty, new names were added to this naming system with the approval of the emperors. Throughout the country all the descendants of Kongzi would act accordingly. During the period of the Republic of China, for the purpose of compiling a universal genealogy of the Kong clan in various places, Kong Lingyi, the Duke of Yansheng of the 76th generation, issued a new naming system for all the members of the Kong clan to follow.

The Kong clan exerted great efforts to compile a genealogy. Revision was done every 30 years while re-compilation was done every 60 years. Strict clan admonitions and family rules were formulated to restrain the conduct of the members of the Kong clan. As the leading branch of the Kong clan, Kong Residence issued *Kong Clan Rules and Regulations* and the clansmen in various places formulated their own family rules and implementing regulations. *Kong Clan Rules and Regulations* admonished the clansmen to pay homage to ancestors, show benevolence, advocate Confucianism, and be courteous and virtuous—all the Confucian moral principles and ethics. On the other hand, the same *Kong Clan Rules and Regulations* restrained women by forcing them to abide by the "three obediences (to their father before marriage, to their husband after marriage and to their son after the death of husband) and to the four virtues (morality, proper speech, modest manner and diligent work)". These spiritual fetters imposed on women resulted in many cases of tragedy in their lives.

Like other surname-based clans, the Kong clan was linked by the ties of blood from the direct paternal line. Confucianism advocated respect to

Right of Primogeniture
According to the feudal system of succession, the right of succession belonged to the eldest son by the wife and not by a concubine.

ancestors. With Kongzi promoted to the status of "sage", his offspring had a stronger sense of family and became more organized. They acted as role models in following Kongzi's instructions. Adopting the patriarchal clan system in ancient China, the Kong clan was dominated by the right of primogeniture—the right of inheritance belonging exclusively to the eldest son. The branch of the eldest son from the direct paternal line was thus considered the main familial branch, whereas all the others were minor branches. The Duke of Yansheng was Kongzi's descendant from the direct paternal line and held the hereditary title of nobility. He assumed heavy responsibility as the head of the Kong clan and governed all the clansmen of the Kong clan. Kong Residence, where the Duke of Yansheng lived, became the symbol of the patriarchal rule.

Kong Residence— Where Inhabitants Are Content with Their Wealth and High Position

Across the Queli street to the east of Kong Temple lies Kong Residence—where Kongzi's offspring of lineal descent lived for generations. From the Song Dynasty through to the Republic of China,

Queli Street

Kongzi's eldest male offspring of lineal descent held the title of the Duke of Yansheng. As a result, Kong Residence was also called "The Duke of Yansheng Residence". The roof of this giant building is covered with grey tiles. Though its area is as large as that of Kong Temple, Kong Residence is no match to the former in respect of the height of their halls.

Kong Residence is known as "the No. 1 residence on earth". The Kong family was a traditional eminent feudal clan and their residence was a huge manor for the nobility. The structure of Kong Residence served as the embodiment of Kongzi thought and traditional Chinese culture. The noble family enjoyed high economic status and political standing. Kong Residence was a combination of government offices and domestic chambers. The middle path was a typical reflection of this phenomenon.

Inaccessible Mansions

When you come out of Kong Temple by the Yucui Gate, you'll step onto the main street in front of Kong Residence. The communications centre of the old city of Qufu will lead you to the door of Kongzi's abode in the west, the Drum Tower Gate in the east and the Bell Tower on the Queli street in the south.

Front Gate of Kong Residence

The Gate of Kong Residence

The Gate of Kong Residence faces a tall white screen wall. This moderately high gate tower still looks solemn and proud. The 12 lotus-shaped meritorious boards on the lintel of the gate clearly demonstrate the high position of the Kong family.

On two sides of the gate stand a pair of stone lions. With a height of 2 metres, they were highly regarded as exquisitely carved works of the Ming Dynasty. The male lion on the east side is playing with a coloured silk ball while the lioness is tenderly fondling her cub in her arms. The opposite lions served as faithful guards and symbolized the awe-inspiring manner of Kong Residence.

The half-a-metre-high square stone in front of the stone lion looks like a bench. It was actually a stepping-stone for mounting a horse. The two-room-deep and

Bell Tower

Inscription Board of "Sage's Residence" at the Top of the Front Gate of Kong Residence

three-room-wide gate is symmetrical in design.

Antithetical Couplet on the Gate

The most eye-catching of the Gate of Kong Residence is the red-framed board hung at the top of the gate inscribed in gold on a blue background with the two characters "sheng fu" (sacred residence). The gate is flanked by an antithetical couplet. Tourists will be fascinated by its neat and graceful calligraphy. The couplet was written by Ji Xiaolan, a famous scholar during the reign of Emperor Qianlong of the Qing Dynasty known as "the No. 1 literary talent on earth". The author earnestly wishes in the couplet that the wealth of the Kong family would be passed on from generation to generation and the literary writings of the Kong family would reach the zenith of perfection. This kind of antithetical couplet could only be written to address the Kong family.

Second Gate of Kong Residence

When you enter the front gate and cross a small courtyard, you'll be faced with the second gate. The four characters "sheng ren zhi men" (the gate of a sage) on the board hanging at the top of the gate were written by Li Dongyang—the Prime Minister of the Ming Dynasty and the father-in-law of Kong Wenshao, Kongzi's descendant of the 62nd generation. The main gate is flanked by two side gates. The six black doors of the three gates look majestic, solemn, ancient and noble. It's no easy job to climb over the half-metre-high threshold. As the social estate system was strictly observed in the Kong family, the main gate was open only to the emperor, imperial envoys and the Duke of Yansheng. All the others, including officials, had to use the side gates. There were originally two Chinese scholar trees in front of the gate. Only one is still standing in the southwest. The tree is so huge that only four people who spread their arms can surround the trunk. This age-old tree is the silent witness of many changes experienced by the Kong family.

The Chongguang Gate

When you go through the second gate, your sight will be blocked by a gate tower standing alone in the middle of the path. The three-door-wide gate is decorated with eight wooden carvings of upside down golden buds. Four black wooden pillars are painted with auspicious clouds, golden dragons and beautiful flowers. During the reign of Emperor Jiajing of the Ming Dynasty, the imperial government decided to build the town of Qufu to safeguard Kong Temple. Emperor Jiajing bestowed the two characters "chong guang" (promote, enhance) to the Kong family, hoping that the

Chongguang Gate

Kong family would carry forward its fine tradition. The Kong family set up this gate with a board decorated with four gold-foiled characters "en ci (betow) chong guang" so as to commemorate this event.

The Chongguang Gate separates the front courtyard and the back courtyard. It is said that the building of this kind of partition gate was not permitted in the residence of ordinary officials. Only officials holding titles of nobility conferred by the emperor enjoyed such privileges. In respect of the Chongguang Gate, its symbolic cultural meaning surpassed its practical meaning. Although the Kong family was granted many titles, only the title of Duke of Yansheng conferred in the Song Dynasty was on a par with the title of nobility. That's why the Kong family was entitled to build such a gate. This gate was only used for such great events as accepting an imperial edict, greeting the arrival of the emperor, holding important festive activities and sacrificial rites. Only then the gate was gradually opened with a 13-gun salvo.

Hanging-Down Decorated Posts

Awe-Inspiring Primary Courtroom

Kong Residence is the decision-making centre controlling the local administrative affairs of Qufu as well as the management centre supervising the domestic affairs of the Kong clan. The official courtroom is the place where the Duke of Yansheng accepted an imperial edict, met with fellow officials, and handled local administrative affairs and domestic affairs of the Kong clan. It was also the office of the officials under its jurisdiction. In addition to the primary courtroom, there were secondary and tertiary courtrooms to its north which had lesser official scopes. The Duke of Yansheng would choose which courtroom to handle his business according to the seniority of the official and the importance of the matter. On both

Indoor Scene of the Primary Courtroom of Kong Residence

sides of the primary courtroom there were altogether six departments—a replica of the six ministries of the central government—and the officials working there took orders from the Duke of Yansheng and served the Kong clan. In actual fact, the courtroom of Kong Residence played the role of a miniature government.

Turning past the Chongguang Gate, you'll find a spacious and pleasant courtyard with a rectangular terrace within it. In front of the terrace, two unique objects will attract your attention. The one on the east side is a coronagraph and the one on the west is a measuring device. A coronagraph was used in ancient times to tell the time, and people in command of the

Weapons and Title Boards Carried by Guards of Honour

time were thought to control everything in the world. All the tributary and vassal states were required to adopt the standard measuring device issued by the central government. For the initial purpose of unifying measures, the measuring device was put there to actually symbolise the unification of government decrees and orders.

Behind the terrace stands a five-room structure. This is none other than the primary courtroom—the most important office of Kong Residence. Hung at the top is an inscription board bestowed by Emperor Shunzhi of the Qing Dynasty. The four inscribed characters "tong she zong xing" (rule the clansmen of the Kong clan) indicate that the power to rule all the clansmen of the Kong clan was granted by the central government to the Kong family.

The primary courtroom was also called the main hall. It was in the main hall that the Duke of Yansheng handled the most important administrative and domestic affairs. The following great events were also held here: the announcement of an imperial edict, the title-conferring ceremony, meetings with high-ranking officials from the central government, the administration of major local incidents and the significant celebrations. On display on the both sides of the main hall are a variety of weapons used by the guard of honour. The long clubs, spears and swords displayed here were used by the guards for the grade-one officials. So from the type of guard of honour, the rank of an official could be distinguished. The guard of honour became

A Group Picture of the Descendants of Kongzi, Mengzi, Yan Hui and Zengzi

the honorary certificate of the Duke of Yansheng. You can imagine the splendour of guard of honour when the Duke of Yansheng made his tour of inspection and went to Beijing on business.

The primary courtroom was the central decision-making organ. The side rooms were occupied by six departments—a replica of the six ministries of the central government. The primary courtroom and six departments combined to form the tight-knit administrative system of the Kong family.

The Department of Land and Revenue was in charge of all the land of the Kong family and the collection of taxes. The head of the department was a Grade-Six official and he had various sections and low-ranking officials under his rule. Local offices outside of Qufu were also set up. The Kong family owned at most a million *mu* of land covering the following five provinces: Shandong, Jiangsu, Anhui, Henan and Hebei. No other noble families could expect to attain so much land.

The Department of Classic Works was in charge of all the ancient historical and cultural classics, thus laying a solid foundation for the home teaching as well as for the cause of education at large. Kong Residence was an important private library.

The Department of Seals was in charge of all the seals and was responsible for signing upon receiving documents.

The Department of Personnel was in charge of all the servants and special craftsmen. The Kong family were engaged in various events and activities. In addition to the permanent servants looking after the routine life of the family members, temporary personnel were in great demand, especially when the sacrificial rites and tomb-sweeping activities were held. The servants of the Kong family had a strict division of labour and their positions could be passed on to their offspring.

The Department of Music was in charge of musical instruments for sacrificial rites and the musicians and dancers.

The Department of Documentation was in charge of registration of all incoming and outgoing official correspondence, records, documents and letters. The existing archives of Kong Residence in Qufu handed down from the past are most valuable historical records.

Solemn Secondary Courtroom

The Secondary Courtroom, which lies to the north of the Primary Courtroom, was also called "back hall". This was the place the Duke of Yansheng met with the grade four and above officials and selected on behalf of the central government the masters of ceremonies for Confucian rituals, musicians and candidates for the primary civil examination.

Inscription Boards in the Secondary Courtroom

There is a narrow corridor linking the Primary Courtroom and the Secondary Courtroom. You can see a bench on each side. It is said that Yan Song, a senior court official during the late period of the Ming Dynasty, once sat on one of the benches. That's why it was called "senior official bench". While in power, Yan Song committed a lot of evil deeds and was finally punished. Yan Song betrothed his granddaughter to Kong Shangxian, Kongzi's descendant of the 64th generation. When his crimes were found out, Yan Song came to Qufu to ask the Duke of Yansheng to plead on his behalf with the emperor. It is said that the Duke of Yansheng was reluctant to meet him and kept him cooling his heels on the bench for a long time. That's why many people called the bench "the cold bench".

In order to discharge the Kong family's obligations of managing local education, the Duke of Yansheng was entrusted by the emperor to conduct examinations in the secondary courtroom for the subjects of rites and music. Smaller than the primary courtroom, the secondary courtroom is decorated with an inscription board bestowed by Emperor Kangxi of the Qing Dynasty. Many works of calligraphy and painting on display were bestowed upon the family by the emperors and the empress

"Longevity" Stone Tablet in the Handwriting of Empress Dowager Cixi Displayed in the Secondary Courtroom

dowagers. The Kong family always had memorial tablets carved to mark each event. You can even find the calligraphic works and paintings of Empress Dowager Cixi, who is a notorious figure in the modern history of China. Her works include the Chinese character "shou" (longevity) in her handwriting and a traditional Chinese painting of "clouds and pines".

There are two smaller rooms on both sides of the secondary courtroom. The one on the east is tantamount to today's receptionist's office. The one on the west was used as both a place of rest and an office for those accompanying officials of the Duke of Yansheng when he planned to make a tour of inspection or go to Beijing on business.

Elegant Tertiary Courtroom

Though small, the courtyard of the tertiary courtroom is well-proportioned and elegant. It has an air of both antiquity and liveliness.

Outdoor Scene of the Tertiary Courtroom

There are two straight and towering Chinese juniper trees on both sides. The Taihu stones of strange shapes and appearances were put in six exquisitely carved stone pots to form beautiful rockery decorations.

The tertiary courtroom, also called "the hall of retreat", served as a reception room for the Kong family. They would meet officials below the rank of grade four and other clansmen here. This was a place where they wrote notes to the throne and handled domestic affairs.

The gold-framed board hanging at the top of the hall is inscribed with the four Chinese characters "liu dai han yi" (six generations enjoy together a sweet life) accompanied by the imperial seal of Emperor Qianlong was bestowed upon the Kong family by the same emperor. In 1757 (the 22nd year of his reign), Emperor Qianlong paid his fourth

Taihu Stones in the Courtyard of the Tertiary Courtroom

visit to Qufu to pay homage to Kongzi. At that time, Madame Huang, the wife of Kong Yuyin (Kongzi's descendant of the 67th generation) was 81 years old, while Kong Xianpei (Kongzi's descendant of the 72nd generation) was already born. From Madame Huang to Kong Xianpei, the six generations lived together and enjoyed a happy life. Impressed by their happy and harmonious life, Emperor Qianlong bestowed the board with these four characters to the Kong family. This is a typical example of how traditional Chinese culture attached great importance to family life.

On display is a calligraphic work of "Rhyme Prose of Post-Chibi" written by Kong Yuyin, Kongzi's descendant of the 67th generation. As Kongzi's descendants of lineal descent, the Dukes of Yansheng were mostly well educated and of high cultural accomplishment. As a result, many calligraphic works, paintings and poems produced by them have become part of the exhibits displayed here.

There are two side rooms in the front of the tertiary courtroom. The one on the east is composed of two rooms. The outer one was used to store all the title deeds for land—part of the important archives of the Kong family. The inner one was in charge of the general affairs and wealth of the Kong family. These two rooms were the places in which the Kong family collected taxes and money by various means. The room on the west is a study, where all the documentation, records and books were sheltered.

A tour of these three courtrooms reveals the political functions of Kong Residence. The residence of the Duke of Yansheng was tantamount to a tributary state in feudal society. In some respects his power surpassed that of the king of a tributary state. He did not handle the trivial local administrative affairs, but was more powerful than a local magistrate.

Gate to the Inner Chambers for Female Members of the Kong Family

After going through the three courtrooms, you'll come across a gate leading to the inner chambers for female members of the Kong family. This moderate gate played a very important role in separating Kong Residence into two different worlds.

As the residence of Kongzi's offspring of lineal descent, Kong Residence acted as a role model in following the Confucian doctrine of distinguishing between the male and female members of the family. The inner chambers were the living quarters of the hosts and all the female members of the family and nobody could enter without permission.

The gate was also called the "forbidden gate". Nobody was allowed to get through this heavily guarded gate without permission. Even important guests were showed in only after his visit was reported to the host and his approval was obtained.

The drinking water used in the inner chambers came from the mountain spring in the east

Gate of the Inner Chambers of Kong Residence

Small Courtyard near the West Corner Door of the Inner Chambers

of Qufu. Every morning, a convoy of carts would transport clear spring water to Kong Residence. As the male servants were not allowed to enter the inner chambers, a hole was made in the wall of the inner chambers. A stone water trough was put up outside the wall near the hole so that the spring water could flow into the pond inside the wall.

When you step into the inner chambers and look backwards, you'll see a picture of an animal on the screen wall. When you glance at it briefly, the eye-catching animal looks like a kylin—a kind of mythical unicorn. However, when you look at it carefully, you'll find an unusual beast with a lion tail, deer antlers and dragon scales. With an open mouth and bared fangs, it has its head raised towards the sun on the upper left side as if it would like to swallow

Hand-Written Directive at the Gate of the Inner Chambers

Picture of a Greedy Beast on the Screen Wall of the Inner Chambers

it whole. The nondescript beast was called "tan", which literally means a "greedy beast". From the picture you can reach the conclusion that the beast was not satisfied with all the treasures around and had a most bizarre idea to swallow the sun. Tradition has it that the greedy beast drowned in the sea in the process of chasing the sun.

The picture was painted on the screen wall before the gate so that everyone would see it before they left the inner chambers. The purpose was to warn the Duke of Yansheng and the rest of Kongzi's offspring against greed. The Duke of Yansheng and his family enjoyed all the benefits of wealth and power, but they still warned themselves against greed. This was

Stone Water Trough

the epitome of the philosophy of life on the part of Kongzi's posterity. Kongzi put morality and justice before material comfort. Confucianism advocated that seeking material gains must be in conformity with morality and justice. If your desire for material comfort was insatiable, you would ruin yourself.

The Front Main Rooms
—A Grand Spectacle of a Big Family

Facing the picture of the greedy beast is the main hall of the front main rooms, where the hosts of Kong Residence gathered together and met with their close relatives and clansmen. As one of the important large halls, the front main hall was often used by the Duke of Yansheng to entertain his close friends and to hold family banquets. Great events such as weddings and funerals were also held here. Sometimes, the front main hall served as a temporary dwelling place for the visiting emperor. For example, Emperor Qianlong of the Qing Dynasty visited Qufu eight times and stayed there many times.

In spring and summer, the air was fragrant with scents from two trees in the south of the courtyard. These two trees and other two dragon-shaped Chinese scholar trees remained green throughout the year and made the courtyard vibrant with life. There was a huge water vat under the trees. The vat was so big that only two people could encircle it with their

Courtyard of the Front Main Rooms

arms outstretched. This served as an important fire prevention facility. In the centre of the courtyard there is a platform made of square bricks. The platform has a stone drum at each corner and was used as a foundation to erect a stage whenever performances were given by the theatrical troupes.

The area of the front main rooms contains seven rooms which are typical of the structure of a sitting room for grade-one officials in the Ming Dynasty. These rooms reflect the grand spectacle of a big family in feudal society. The central scroll hung in the middle of the wall is a giant Chinese character "shou" (longevity) written by Empress Dowager Cixi. There are several antithetical couplets presented by the famous personages of the Republic of China to Kong Lingyi and his son Kong Decheng. The tables and chairs in the main hall are made of precious *nanmu* wood. The first

Indoor Scene of the Front Main Rooms

room on the east side is furnished with a bed and several chairs bestowed upon the Duke of Yansheng by Emperor Qianlong of the Qing Dynasty. The great variety of exquisite furniture, cultural relics and rare antiques in the room are a feast for the eyes. The east side room is furnished with a bed and several chairs bestowed upon the Kong family by Emperor Qianlong of the Qing Dynasty. On display on the desk is the original imperial edict issued by Emperor Tongzhi. You can also see a collection of cloisonné enamel with bright colours and plain patterns made in the Ming Dynasty. In the west room where Kong Lingyi, the Duke of Yansheng, used to read and sign documents, you'll see a desk covered with four treasures of the study—writing brush, ink stick, ink slab and paper—and a bookshelf lined with Confucian classics and the genealogy of the Kong clan.

Outdoor Scene of the Front Storied House

There are five additional rooms on each wing for storing the sacrificial vessels and for keeping accounts.

Front Storied House
—Living Quarters for a Big Family

Situated behind the front main hall is the front storied house where the Duke of Yansheng Kong Lingyi, Kongzi's descent of 76th generation, lived. This is a fine example of living quarters for the nobility in feudal China.

The front two-storied house consists of seven rooms on each floor and is the main living quarters in the inner chambers. The eight lofty

Indoor Scene of the Front Storied House

black pillars stand as high as the top of the second floor. The courtyard in front of the house is flanked by two smaller storied houses. The east one was inhabited by internal butlers and also served as a storeroom for refreshments, sweets and gifts at the service of the hosts. The west one was the lodging of the senior stewards.

The front storied house is arranged exactly as it was when Kong Lingyi lived there. You'll be attracted by the horizontal inscription board hung at the top and an antithetical couplet at its sides. Feng Shu, a scholar in the Qing Dynasty, wrote the antithetical couplet to eulogize the host of the Kong family for observing the instructions of his ancestors and carrying forward the traditions of poetry and rites.

The first room to the east, beside the small central lounge was the living room of Kong Lingyi. The inner east room was the bedroom of his wife Madame Tao. Kong Lingyi's first wife, Madame Sun, died early and he married the daughter of a high-ranking official in Beijing. His second wife, Madame Tao, took charge of Kong Residence in the late period of its history. The innermost room was the bedroom of his two daughters–Kong Deqi and Kong Demao.

The first room to the west was the bedroom of Wang Baocui, Kong Decheng's biological mother. Wang Baocui was a maid whom Madame Tao brought to Kong Residence with her when she was married to Kong Lingyi. Madame Tao once gave birth to a baby, but unfortunately, the baby died and Madame Tao was unable to have any more children. As a result, Kong Lingyi took Wang Baocui as his concubine. Madame Wang gave birth to Kong Deqi, Kong Demao and Kong Decheng. She died shortly after her only son, Kong Decheng, was born.

The second room to the west was the bedroom of Madame Feng, another of Kong Linglyi's wives. Madame Feng remained obscure and died quite young.

The arrangement of the bedrooms for his three wives demonstrated the hierarchy of women in a feudal society in China. In a house, the rooms on the east were considered superior to the ones on the west. So far as the rooms on the same side are concerned, the central one was superior to the outer ones. That's why Madame Tao occupied the central bedroom, closest to Kong Lingyi's bedroom. Though a mother of

Portrait of Madame Wang, Kong Decheng's Biological Mother

Bedroom of Madame Wang, Kong Decheng's Biological Mother

three children, Wang Baocui was a concubine of a humble origin and had to live in a west bedroom. Madame Feng, having the lowest social status of the three, was accommodated in the corner bedroom on the west.

Rear Storied House
—Impressive Manner for a Big Family

The storied house lying to the rear of the front storied house was inhabited by Kong Lingyi's son, Kong Decheng, before he left China's mainland. The father living in the front house and his son living to the rear demonstrated a typical example of the traditional relationship between

Outdoor Scene of the Back Storied House

father and son—the latter following the former.

Kong Decheng, styled as Dasheng, was born on the fourth day of the first month in 1920 according to the Chinese lunar calendar, several months after his father Kong Lingyi, the Duke of Yansheng, had died of illness. In April 1920, the title of the Duke of Yansheng was conferred on him. He was to be the last Duke of Yansheng in Chinese history. In 1935 his title was replaced by that of "dacheng zhisheng fengsi guan" (special official in charge of offering sacrifices to the greatest sage and teacher Kongzi). From the day he was born to 1937—when the Japanese army invaded Shangdong— Kong Decheng lived in the inner chambers of Kong Residence. In 1937 he moved to Nanjing and later went to Taiwan together with the Nationalist Party of China. He was the head of the Examination Council there before his

Eaves at the Northwest Corner of the Back Storied House

retirement. After he retired, he became the executive council member of Taiwan Society of Confucius and Mencius.

The rear storied house shared the same architectural style as the front storied house— two stories with seven rooms on each floor.

Wedding Picture of Kong Decheng and Sun Qifang

It originally served as the living quarters of the mother of the Duke of Yansheng. However, on December 16, 1936 Kong Decheng made his bridal chamber here when he, a 16-year-old sacrificial official, married Sun Qifang, the granddaughter of Sun Jia'nai—No. 1 Scholar of the late Qing Dynasty. The bridal chamber is still arranged as it was when they got married.

Hung in the middle of the main living room is the red Chinese character "xi" (double happiness) embroidered with the patterns of peonies. The peony, which is regarded one of China's national flowers, symbolizes wealth and good luck. You can find a red sheet of silk sent as a gift by Lin Sen, Chairman of the Nationalist government, with the congratulatory message written on it wishing the newlyweds a happy marriage.

The room is also decorated with congratulatory antithetical couplets presented by other high-ranking officials, famous personages such as Shen Honglie and Xu Yongchang. The works of calligraphy and painting and red-silk-covered chairs complement each other, thus creating a warm festive atmosphere.

The first room to the east was the living room of Kong Decheng. Hung on the east wall was a scroll painting of peonies presented as a gift by Mei Lanfang, one of the most famous Beijing opera performers. The painting of beautiful peonies with luxuriant foliage and spreading branches was painted by Mei Lanfang himself. The two inner rooms were the bedroom of Kong Decheng and his wife and that of his son Kong Weiyi and daughter Kong Wei'e. A picture of Kong Decheng, his wife and their two children was hung on the wall. The west room was the bedroom of Kong Decheng's wet nurse. It is said Kong Decheng continues to miss her for her loving care.

The front courtyard is flanked by two small storied houses. The east one was an embroidery room used by the female members of the Kong family. On display here are the daily necessities of maids, embroidery implements and some works of embroidery. The west one served as a guest room for visiting female relatives.

All these two-storied houses combine to form a square courtyard. The veranda of the front house protrudes above. Four pomegranate trees are planted there. As a pomegranate has a lot of seeds and its Chinese pronunciation can also mean "stay", pomegranates are planted here to imply that the Kong family will have a lot of sons to carry forward the family's name.

There is a small courtyard behind the rear storied house. The rear five rooms here are not comparable to the majestic and luxurious rooms in the rear storied house. These plain rooms served as the dormitory for maid servants. This part was called "zao (jujube) huai (Chinese scholar tree) xuan (hall)" because jujube trees and Chinese scholar trees were originally planted in the courtyard. Nowadays, it has become an exhibition space used to display the portraits of

Group Picture of Kong Decheng and His Wife and Children

Kongzi's offspring of lineal descent and their life stories, as well as the portraits of famous personages from Qufu in Chinese history.

A Scholarly Family of Lofty Morality

The buildings along the three paths played different roles and the east and west paths served as a foil for the central path where the Duke of Yansheng Residence was situated. The Mu'en Hall, Baoben Hall and Yiguan Hall on the east path were the embodiment of Kongzi's offspring's maintenance of the fine tradition of showing respect and offering sacrifices to their ancestors. The Hong'e Veranda, Zhong Shu Hall, An Huai Hall and the Study on the west path are where the Duke of Yansheng pursued his studies and met with guests. According to the values of the Chinese intelligentsia, gaining fame by writing and becoming a role model in moral integrity is a life-long pursuit. This was also the typical goal of a scholarly family of lofty morality.

The East Path of Kong Residence —Morality-Themed East Complex

The structures along the east path of Kong Residence are called the east complex, which covers one third of its total area. Some original buildings were ruined by the end of the Qing Dynasty. However, the existing structures are well preserved.

The main buildings of the east complex were built to manifest Confucian doctrines. The Mu'en Hall gave expression to their loyalty and gratitude to the emperor. The Baoben Hall embodied their respect and filial piety to their ancestors. The Yiguan Hall reflected the harmony and amiability between brothers.

The Sightseeing Terrace

There is an earthen terrace at the southern end of the east complex. Standing on the terrace you can appreciate the scenes outside Kong Residence.

The sightseeing terrace was not included in the original design of Kong Residence. In feudal society the female members of a noble family were not supposed to go out at will. Even if festive events were held outside, they were still secluded within the high walls.

For their convenience, the Kong family built this earth terrace and put up a shed where the female members could view the sights outside from within the confines of the residence, hence the name of "sightseeing terrace".

The Mu'en Hall

Adjacent to the middle of the east path there is a courtyard. The five-room hall in the north is called the Mu'en Hall or Bao'en Hall. This ancestral hall was built to commemorate Madame Yu, wife of the Duke of Yansheng Kong Xianpei—Kongzi's descent of the 72nd generation.

Madame Yu was the daughter of Emperor Qianlong of the Qing

Dynasty. There is a tale of how the princess made it possible to marry a member of the Kong family. Tradition has it that Madame Yu had a mole on her face. According to the fortune-teller, she should be married into a family of nobility. The Kong family had at this time been a noble family for about 2000 years. However, the imperial family was of Manchu nationality while the Duke of Yansheng was of Han nationality. The established conventions prevented marriage between these two nationalities. They cleverly mapped out a scheme. The imperial family gave away the princess to Yu Minzhong, a grade-two official of Han nationality, as his adoptive daughter. Then, as Yu Minzhong's daughter, she was able to marry the Duke of Yansheng Kong Xianpei. After their marriage, the imperial government offered the Kong family unprecedented benefits and privileges. The Kong family built the Mu'en Hall to show their gratitude to the emperor and princess. They held sacrificial rites there.

The courtyard where the Mu'en Hall stands is not symmetrical in its layout. That was the proposal of a *feng shui* (geomancy) master.

The Baoben Hall

The Baoben Hall was the private temple of the Kong family. When Kongzi's offspring of lineal descent died, his memorial tablet would be placed in this temple. Kong Temple was tantamount to a national temple, so the sacrificial rites held there were regarded as national events. When the Kong family offered sacrifices to Kongzi or other ancestors in the Baoben Hall, the ceremony was considered as a family event. In the celebration of Kongzi's birthday, other festivities and events, the Duke of Yansheng would hold sacrificial rites in the private family temple. They would load the table before the memorial tablets of their ancestors with pork, lamb and other offerings before reading an elegiac address. The sacrificial rite was

A Bird's-Eye View of the Yiguan Hall

hosted by the Duke of Yansheng himself. If he was unable to appear on the occasion, he would appoint the head of the Kong clan to take his place.

The Yiguan Hall

The Yiguan Hall, which lies behind the Mu'en Hall, was the biggest building in the east complex and the only one used as living quarters.

The Yiguan Hall consisted of two five-room houses. The north house had two cosy balconies across which ran a railing. This house was the living quarters of the eldest younger brother of the Duke of Yansheng. The name "yi guan", quoted from *The Analects of Confucius*, means "A basic idea (benevolance) runs through the entire Confucian teachings." The hall was so named to show the idea of benevolence and kind-heartedness advocated and carried out by Kongzi and his offspring.

Lookout Tower

A small building standing in the middle of the east path and facing the gate of the inner chambers is called the Lookout Tower. The building, which looks more like a watchtower, was built in the late period of the Ming Dynasty. The four-metre-wide building is 20 metres high. Standing at the top you can enjoy a view into the distance. The square, four-storied tower was built of large rectangular bricks. The upper two floors have windows on four sides while the first floor has windows on three sides. There is only one door facing north on the windowless ground floor. The door was wrapped with an iron plate and is strong enough to withstand fire. The lookout tower is near the gate of the inner chambers. If the inner chambers were attacked by bandits, the Duke of Yansheng and his family could climb up to the tower to take refuge. That's why this tower was also called the "refuge tower".

Refuge Tower

The West Path of Kong Residence —Study-Themed West Complex

The structures along the west path of Kong Residence are called the west complex. During the reign of Emperor Daoguang, the west complex was called the "west study". As the concrete embodiment of the fact that the Kong family attached importance to learning, the west study was built to provide a venue for members of the Kong family to read classics and cultivate themselves. The Duke of Yansheng made use of the west complex to meet with visitors, pursue learning, write poems and practise rites. The west complex consists of more than 90 rooms, which are connected by long corridors. With many trees and flowers planted there, the courtyards seem quiet and secluded. Many rooms are decorated with works of calligraphy, paintings and antithetical couplets.

The Hong'e Veranda

The Hong'e Veranda, which is located in the fourth courtyard, was built during the reign of Emperor Qianlong of the Qing Dynasty. The veranda has wooden pillars under eaves, and a bench against a railing. The windows and doors are decorated with exquisitely carved lattices. The veranda is flanked by two rooms. There is a terrace to the front and a rockery close to the south wall. At the southwest corner of the courtyard stands a towering tree. The Hong'e Veranda was the place where the Duke of Yansheng read classics and met with visitors. He devoted himself to the pursuit of learning and self-cultivation by reading many classical works written by previous sages and scholars. In between his reading, he liked to sit on the wooden bench and feast his eyes on the beautiful sight of the fragrant garden. In this

Indoor Scene of Hong'e Veranda

Outdoor Scene of Hong'e Veranda

way he refreshed himself and cultivated his mind.

The Zhong Shu Hall

The Zhong Shu Hall faces a square courtyard behind the Hong'e Veranda. The three golden characters "zhong shu tang" on a board hung

Zhong Shu (Loyalty and Forbearance)

In Chinese "zhong", which means faithfulness and loyalty, is regarded as the principle which guides interpersonal relationships. "Shu" implies the meaning of "putting oneself in the place of another". One should do onto others as one would be done by. One would not be respected unless one respects others. As a whole, "zhong shu", means "benevolence" and "benevolent government". It is looked upon as a way in which one embarks on a political career and the way one ought to conduct oneself in society. Hence, it is an integral part of Confucianism.

Outdoor Scene of the Zhong Shu Hall

inside at the top were written by the Duke of Yansheng Kong Yuyin, Kongzi's descent of the 67th generation. Kong Yuyin was invited to be the teacher of Emperor Yongzheng. The Zhong Shu Hall was the place where Kong Yuyin studied. Succeeding Dukes of Yansheng made use of this place to learn poetry and rites, train in refined styles of conversation and practise the code of conduct. The name "zhong shu", quoted from *The Analects of Confucius*, means "loyalty and forbearance". This is an excellent complement to the Yiguan Hall in the east complex.

There are rooms on both sides of the courtyard. Stone table and chairs were put on the terrace. Two large banyans and one pomegranate tree adorn the courtyard.

The An Huai Hall

The five-room-wide An Huai Hall boasts exquisite carving and partition. The board hung at the top is inscribed with three Chinese characters "an huai tang" written in running calligraphic style.

Right: Indoor Scene of the Zhong Shu Hall

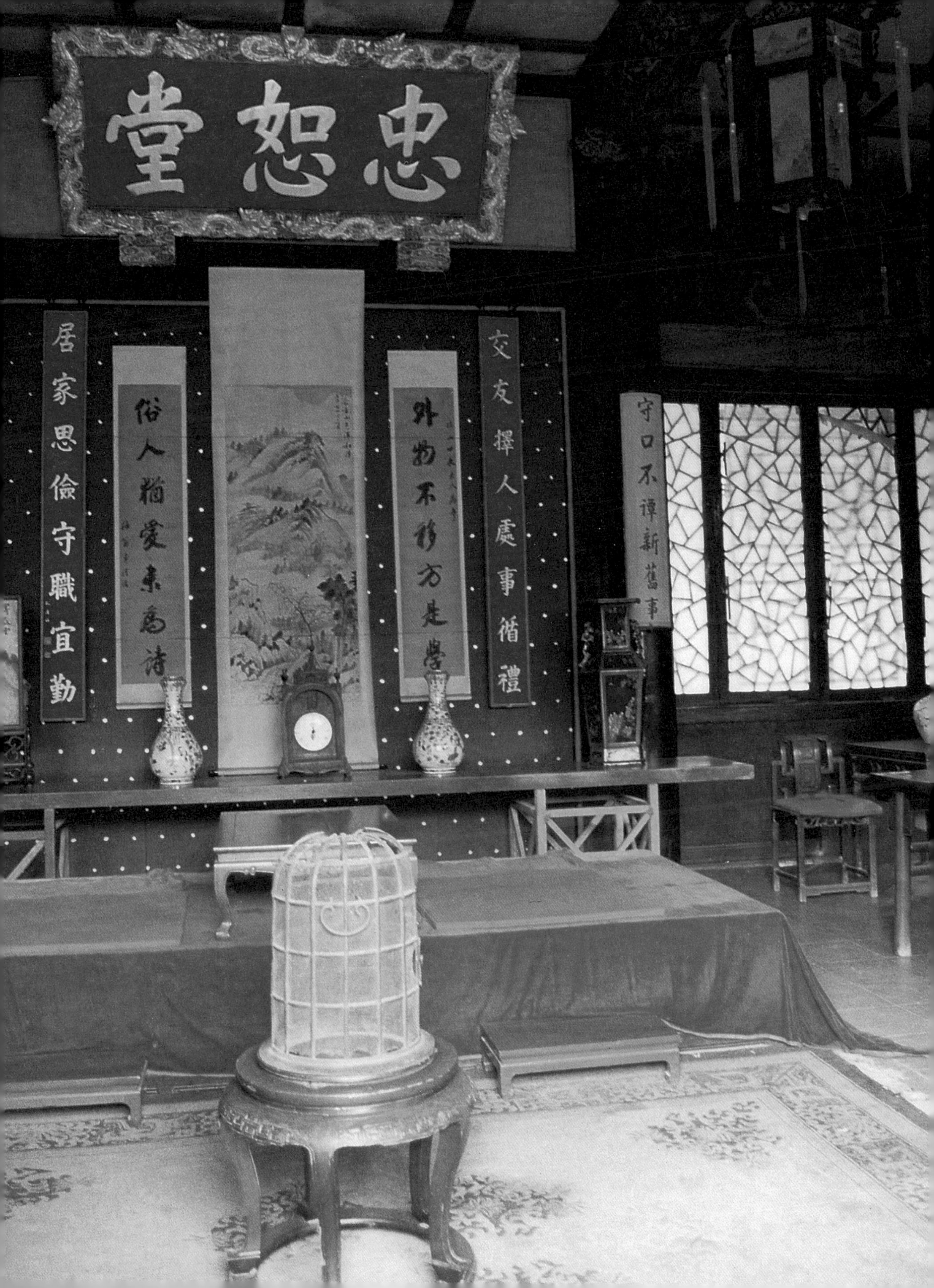
忠恕堂
居家思儉守職宜勤
交友擇人處事循禮
俗人猶愛未為詩
外物不移方是學
守口不譚新舊事

Outdoor Scene of the An Huai Hall

Bamboo Grove behind the An Huai Hall

Unlike traditional architectural design, the An Huai Hall is not symmetrical. Different shapes of rooms are put together, such as horizontal rooms, vertical rooms, round suites, suites composed of big and small rooms. A great variety of different doors can be seen here: rectangular doors, round doors, long doors, hexagonal doors, oval doors and grape-trellis doors. Such an unusual layout is closely connected with its name. The name "an huai", quoted from *The Analects of Confucius*, reflects the ideal society Kongzi longed for—a stable society where the elderly will be provided for and the young

Outdoor Scene of the Drawing Hall

will be properly cared for. The rooms and doors in various shapes are meant to denote complex and diversified social phenomena. The human society, though of infinite variety, is moving towards the ideal society of great harmony. This lofty ideal of humankind accords with everyone's long-cherished wish and fundamental interests.

Drawing Halls

There are two drawing halls behind the An Huai Hall. The 7.2-metre-high south drawing hall has a north veranda, while the 8.2-metre-high north drawing hall has a south veranda. The two drawing halls, which consist of three rooms each, are symmetrical. The An Huai Hall is connected with the two drawing halls in a disorderly way. Unlike the luxurious halls along the middle path of Kong Residence, the two drawing halls are decorated in a simple but elegant style. Many plants are grown in the courtyard, such as pomegranate, bajiao banana, papaya, crab-apple and wintersweet. When they bloom, the courtyard decked out with luxuriant foliage and flowers is a blaze of colours. This scene, together with unusual Taihu stones, green bamboos and fragrant magnolia, makes the place tranquil and elegant. If you come here in sultry summer, you'll find this place an ideal summer resort you can't tear yourself away from.

Inner Study

The three rooms to the rear of the north drawing hall are the "inner study" of the Kong family. You can find the memorial tablet of Kongzi in the middle of the study. Actually, the memorial tablet of Kongzi was set up in all the public and private schools in ancient China. To Kongzi's offspring, home learning was an important means of acquiring the knowledge about poetry, classics, rites and music. Thanks to this fine tradition of home learning, brilliant scholars emerged in succession among Kongzi's descendants.

Back Garden

Walking out of the Zaohuai Veranda on the middle path of Kong Residence and turning backwards, you'll find a great stretch of open garden. The garden is distinguished by pavilions and verandas, tiny bridges and small creeks, singing birds and fragrant flowers. At the sight of this pleasant

Back Garden or Tieshan Garden

garden, you will feel relaxed and refreshed. This is the back garden of Kong Residence, which is also called "Tieshan Garden". The garden, which lies to the rear of the inner chambers, the east complex and the west complex, is a replica of an imperial garden. The hosts of Kong Residence used to enjoy their leisure in this picturesque garden.

The essence of Chinese gardening culture is good taste. A symmetric design should be avoided. The principal taste is naturalness. The layout of pavilions, terraces and towers should be designed by bringing topographical advantages into full play. Emphasis should be laid on the emotional communication between man and nature. The back garden of Kong Residence is characteristic of these features. Being a garden of a noble family in the north, the back garden also bears the styles of gardens in the south. Such a harmonious combination of two different styles is rarely seen in the north of China.

The History of Tieshan Garden

The back garden is the biggest of many gardens owned by the Duke of Yansheng in Qufu. It was first built in 1503 (the 16th year of the reign of Emperor Hongzhi of the Ming Dynasty).

The back garden was also called Tieshan (iron hill) Garden because there were several blocks of iron ore, the biggest being three metres long and two metres wide. Tradition has it that several aerolites fell into the ground from the sky during the reign of Emperor Jiaqing of the Qing Dynasty. The aerolites grew up like bamboo shoots from wood into iron. The scenario symbolized that fortune was smiling at the Kong family. The Duke of Yansheng Kong Qingrong, Kongzi's descendant of the 73rd generation, believed the magic aerolites coming from outer space would reinvigorate the Kong family and named the back garden "Tieshan Garden". He styled himself as "the Host of the Tieshan Garden".

In actual fact, the iron ores were not aerolites at all. An archaeological excavation of the ancient city of the Lu Kingdom discovered iron ores of the same chemical composition. This demonstrated that the iron ores found in the back garden were the result of iron-smelting in ancient times or were moved into the garden from outside of the city. Although the iron ores were sham aerolites, the high artistic attainments obtained by the Host of the Tieshan Garden, Kong Qingrong, were genuine. *The Poetry of Tieshan Garden* and *The Paintings of Tieshan Garden* published by him were considered masterpieces. He liked to make friends with famous

Rockery, Fan-Shaped Pavilion and Zigzag Bridge

personages throughout the country. He invited them to be his guests. They did paintings, wrote poems and drank liquor together at Kong Residence. It is said that Kong Qingrong drank like a fish and was known as the No. 3 heavy drinker among the literary scholars.

A Paradise for the Members of the Kong Family Living in the Inner Chambers of Kong Residence

The garden of Kong Residence underwent three major renovations

and several minor repairs. The garden was expanded with each renovation and finally covered an area of dozens of *mu*. The garden was arranged and decorated with hills, water, forest, zigzag bridges, sunken flower-beds, waterside pavilions and fountains. In addition, there were stone islands surrounded by water, a drawing room for enjoying the cool, a stone altar for worshipping the god of flowers, a veranda for watching the bright moon, and a platform study for reading after burning joss sticks. When you relax in the pavilions and saunter amidst fragrant flowers, you'll find it difficult to tear yourself away from Tieshan Garden. It goes without saying that the back garden was a paradise for the Duke of Yansheng and the members of the Kong family living in the inner chambers of Kong Residence.

Besides waterside pavilions there are rockeries and a variety of plants. Every time the garden was renovated, more unusual stones, famous flowers and special plants were moved in. You can find Japanese flowering cherry and nasturtium given as gifts by Japanese friends. Today's garden presents a most refined and pleasant sight.

There is a unique scene at the centre of the garden. A Chinese scholar tree is tightly encircled by five cypresses, hence the name "five cypresses embracing a Chinese scholar tree". Though 500 years old, the towering tree is still growing with luxuriant foliage and spreading branches.

The rockery at the southeast corner of the garden was built of stones and rocks moved from various parts of China since the Ming and Qing Dynasties. You will be attracted by a fan-shaped pavilion. The hosts of Kong Residence often enjoyed themselves there by observing fish and drinking liquor. Nowadays, the back garden has become a popular tourist attraction for both Chinese and foreign travellers.

Left: Chinese Scholar Tree Embraced by Five Cypresses

Kong Forest
—No. 1 Forest on Earth

Kong Forest is not only the biggest, most long-lasting and best preserved family cemetery in China and in the world, but also a huge man-made forest of a size rarely seen on earth. The first grave was made of the earth brought by Kongzi's disciples in handfuls. At present, Kong Forest covers an area of more than 180 hectares and contains over 100,000 graves.

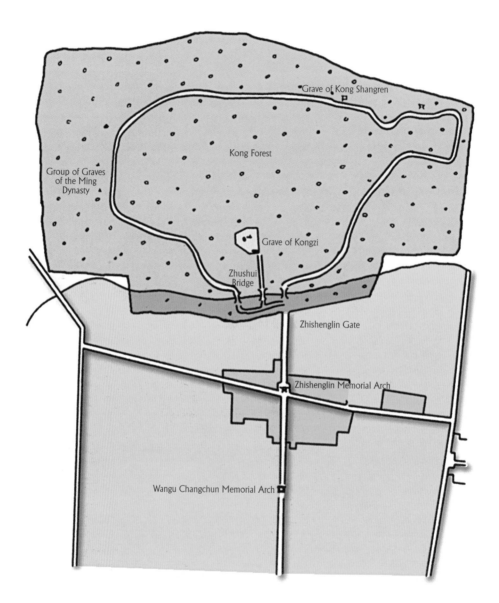

Grave of Kong Shangren

Kong Forest

Group of Graves
of the Ming
Dynasty

Grave of Kongzi

Zhushui
Bridge

Zhishenglin Gate

Zhishenglin Memorial Arch

Wangu Changchun Memorial Arch

A Map of Kong Forest

China's ancient architectural culture includes four main types: palaces, temples, gardens and graves. Kong Temple and Kong Residence are the concentrated manifestation of the architectural features of palaces, temples and gardens. Kong Forest is the combination of the function of graves and the styles of gardens. Kong Temple and Kong Residence demonstrate the extensiveness and profundity of Kongzi thought and the dignity and solemnity of the Kong family. Kong Forest, on the other hand, reflects the honour and glory Kongzi and his offspring enjoyed after their death.

A Brief Account of Kong Forest

There is a rectangular forest belt stretching from east to west at a place 1.5 kilometres to the north of the city of Qufu. Kongzi, the famous thinker and educator in ancient China, was buried there. His descendants were buried around his grave. With the passage of time, Kong Forest—the family cemetery of the Kong clan—came into being. Numerous graves, plentiful stone tablets and towering ancient trees combine to make Kong Forest not only the biggest, most long-lasting and best preserved family cemetery in China and in the world, but also a huge man-made forest of a size rarely seen on earth. The first grave was made of the earth brought by Kongzi's disciples in handfuls. At present, Kong Forest covers an area of more than 180 hectares and contains over 100,000 graves. This is the concrete

Painting of the Sage's Life

embodiment of the fact that various dynasties in Chinese history showed respect to Kongzi and the Kong family.

The Sage Passed Away

Sima Qian, the famous historian and the author of *Historical Records*, devoted one chapter to the introduction of Kongzi. According to him, Kongzi was buried by the side of the Sishui River in the north of the Lu Kingdom.

Historical Records

Historical Records was written by Sima Qian during the reign of Emperor Wu of the Western Han Dynasty. This was the first comprehensive history of China. The 130-volume book recorded a history of 3000 years from the legendary Yellow Emperor to Emperor Wu of the Western Han Dynasty. Drawing abundant materials and covering a variety of subjects, this earnestly-written book is a valuable source book for the study of ancient Chinese history.

A Map of Kong Forest Left Over from the Ming Dynasty

Kongzi was the greatest sage of his time. He gained a deep insight into the society and human life. He had his own understanding of the mandate of heaven, ghosts and spirits. Kongzi suffered many setbacks in his life, but he constantly strove forward, even in adversity. Kongzi held the opinion that as long as one was confident that one's struggle conformed to the will of heaven, one should not be discouraged even if forced to endure hardships. Kongzi loved the natural life of a human being, and also set high store by the spiritual value of a human being.

Kongzi maintained that sacrificial rites should be adopted to educate people on how to bear in memory the merits and virtues of their ancestors. To him, the sacrificial rite was the continuation of the spiritual value of a human being. That's why Kongzi exalted the Duke of Zhou for his rites. He

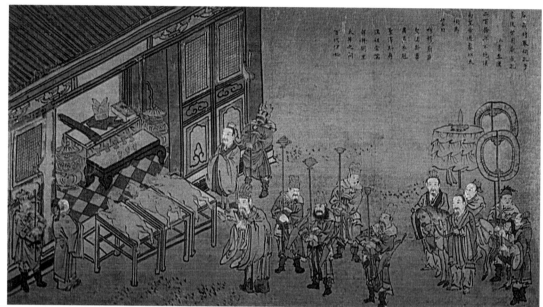

Painting of Emperor Gaozu of the Han Dynasty Offering Sacrifices to Kongzi

attached great importance to burial and regarded burial as the foundation of the patriarchal and hierarchical system. He advocated that everyone should be buried according to the ritual regulations.

The History of Kong Forest

When Kongzi passed away, his disciple Zigong built a shed at the side of his grave to keep vigil. This marked the beginning of the construction of Kong Forest. Kongzi advocated benevolent government, but his ideas were rejected by many rulers of states during the Spring and Autumn Period when rites and music were ignored and wars were unleashed one after another. Although Kongzi was well known for his cultivation of many talented students, his death did not command wide attention. Only the Duke of Ai of the Lu Kingdom wrote an elegiac article to pay respects to

Wall of Kong Forest

him. There was only a six-foot square memorial altar in front of his grave. No memorial tablet was erected. Not a single memorial structure was built.

This situation did not change until the Han Dynasty. In the early period of the Han Dynasty, Kongzi was looked up to as *Su Wang*, a king not enthroned, who had helped the Han Dynasty formulate the rules of law. Kongzi was considered a man who had the virtues of a king, but did not hold the title of a king. Liu Bang, Emperor Gaozu of the Han Dynasty, offered sacrifices to Kongzi himself, thus marking the beginning of a new historical era in which the emperors of various dynasties would show respect to and pay homage to Kongzi. Emperor Wu of the Han Dynasty paid supreme tribute to Confucianism while banning all other schools of thought. Kongzi and Confucianism began to acquire a dominant position in the realm of ideology. Ever since then, the rulers of various dynasties held grand sacrificial rites in memory of Kongzi when they worshipped heaven and earth. Priority was given to the building and renovation of Kongzi's grave.

A Bird's-Eye View of Kong Forest

The ancient Chinese grave culture laid emphasis on the height, width, depth and solemnity of the grave. A grave was usually built on a mountain or a hill surrounded by towering pines and cypresses in order to demonstrate its height. A grave tended to cover a large area in order to display its great size. The sacred ways leading to a grave were to be several kilometres long and sometimes were divided into a main way and a minor way in order to emphasize its depth. Ancient trees, stone figures, stone animals, ornamental columns, altar tables and stone tablets combined to show its solemnity. This kind of architectural design was intended to intensify the visitor's sense of grandeur and solemnity. Anyone who has visited Kong Forest will no doubt have gained a deep impression.

The Sacred Way Linking Two Worlds

Outside the north gate of Qufu there is a 1.5 kilometre, ancient tree-lined path leading to Kong Forest. This is "the sacred way leading to Kongzi, the greatest sage and teacher". People call it "the sacred way leading to Kong Forest" for sake of ease.

To the minds of ancient people, a sacred way links the secular society and the supernatural world. The sacred way is the path Kongzi takes when he comes out of the grave to attend the sacrificial rites. The sacred way is

Sacred Way of Kong Forest

lined in an orderly way with age-old juniper trees and cypresses. The green foliage of the trees makes the ancient sacred way full of life and vitality. Some trees seem to represent the aged people who have experienced many generations of life and are still loyal and faithful to Kongzi by standing guard for an age.

Halfway along the sacred way is a bridge called the "Wenjin Bridge". When you cross the bridge and walk northwards, you'll find the Wangu Changchun Memorial Arch. There is a stele pavilion on each side of the memorial arch. The stone tablet in the west pavilion is inscribed to describe the process of renovating the temple of Kong Forest. The stone tablet in the east pavilion is the landmark of the sacred way.

Wangu Changchun Memorial Arch

The Wangu Changchun Memorial Arch

Behind the Wenjin Bridge stands an exquisitely designed stone memorial arch–the Wangu Changchun Memorial Arch—one of the most famous memorial arches in China. This arch was built in 1594 (the 22nd year of the reign of Emperor Wanli of the Ming Dynasty), and is the biggest and most refined of existing stone arches in Qufu. On each side of the arch there is a stele pavilion built in the Ming Dynasty. The green-tiled square pavilion faces south. The entire arch, complemented by the stele pavilions, looks all the more dignified and stately.

Kongzi thought has influenced one generation of Chinese people after

Stone Carvings in Relief of the Wangu Changchun Memorial Arch

Shenglin Gate

another for around 2000 years and the people of today continue to draw nourishment from Kongzi thought. The name of the arch facing the main gate of Kong Forest—"wan gu chang chun" (remain fresh forever)—implies that Kongzi thought will remain as vital as the pine and cypress and last forever.

Forest Gate

At the end of the sacred way stands the main gate of Kong Forest. Local people simply call it the "forest gate". Covered with green tiles and upturned eaves, the five-beam, three-room gate looks like a decorated arch over a gateway. The forest gate was first built in 1332 (the 3rd year of the reign of Emperor Zhishun of the Yuan Dynasty) and was renovated in the Ming and Qing Dynasties. A wooden memorial arch was established in front of the gate and the board hung at the top was carved with three characters "zhi sheng lin" (the forest of the greatest sage). The memorial arch was first built in 1424 (the 22nd year of the reign of Emperor Yongle of the Ming Dynasty) and was renovated in the Qing Dynasty. The memorial arch and the forest gate complement each other and make this place look all the more dignified and solemn.

Second Forest Gate

When you enter the forest gate, you'll step onto a 400-metre-long path leading to the second forest gate. The deep and serene path is lined with verdant pines and cypresses. The second forest gate is formally called "zhi sheng lin men lou" (the arch over a gateway of the forest of the greatest sage), but is casually called "second forest gate" or even "second gate". The second forest gate consists of two layers. The lower layer is a five-room and double-eave arched gate. The two red-painted doors are inlaid with 81 (9×9) decorative flower-patterned nails. This symbolized the noble status of Kongzi. The upper layer is a horizontal stone tablet inscribed with three characters "zhi sheng lin" (the forest of the greatest sage) in seal cutting. The gate was first built in the Yuan Dynasty. Then, during the reign of Emperor Hongzhi of the Ming Dynasty, an observation tower called "guan lou" was erected on the gate.

The protruding part between the front gate and the second gate is like the outer walled city in an ancient city. Only after you pass the second forest gate can you truly say you've entered Kong Forest.

Stone Lion

Unrivalled Man-Made Forest

After climbing up 36 brick steps, you'll reach the observation tower. From here you'll get a bird's-eye view of an immense forest and will be wowed by beautiful scenes of Kong Forest.

Tradition has it that after Kongzi passed away, his disciples brought saplings of the trees growing in their home towns and planted them around Kongzi's grave. This marked the beginning of tree-planting in Kong Forest. As a result of persistent efforts made from generation to generation, a forest came into being during the Northern and Southern Dynasties. The principal types of trees in Kong Forest include juniper, cypress, Chinese pistachio, toothed oak, elm, and Chinese magnolia. According to statistics, there are more than 40,000 big trees planted after the Song Dynasty, including over 9,000 ancient trees. These ancient trees are more than 100 years old and the oldest ones are over 1,000 years old.

Kong Forest was renovated and expanded during all the dynasties after the Han Dynasty. Its expansion did not end until the period when China was under the reign of Emperor Kangxi. At that time Kong Forest covered an area of over 3,000 *mu* (183.3 hectares). Kong Forest was surrounded by a 7.25-kilometre brick wall with a height of three metres and a thickness of 1.5 metres. The existing 40-plus halls, pavilions, archways and gateways, which consist of 116 rooms, were built during the Ming and Qing Dynasties. Kong Forest assumes the shape of a west-east rectangle. Kongzi's grave is situated south of the centre and his offspring have been buried around his grave in good order. Of more than 100,000 graves built in the different periods of Chinese history, the best-known are the graves of Kongzi, his sons and grandsons, the ancestor of resurgence Kong Renyu,

Grave of Kongzi's Parents

various Dukes of Yansheng and other famous personages.

Numerous trees and verdant grasses make Kong Forest a favourable environment for many types of plants. Take medicinal plants for example, there are as many as 150 types in Kong Forest. Alpine yarrow, Chinese pistachio and glossy ganoderma are known as the "three treasures of Kong Forest" endowed by nature.

Kong Forest is like a museum of natural history. Its long history, rich cultural relics and favourable ecological environment are important material objects in the study of China's ancient society—its politics, economy, culture and burial customs.

Zhushui Bridge

The Essence of Kong Forest—from Zhushui Bridge to the Grave of Kongzi

The rectangular wall of Kong Forest is seven kilometres long. Built of grey bricks, the wall will leave a deep impression on the visitors as a place of eternal serenity. Inside the wall is a ring road paved with stones. The circular road is as long as five kilometres. The combination of an outer rectangle and an inner circle is the embodiment of traditional Chinese culture. To the south of the centre of the ring road is a courtyard encircled by a red wall. This is the place of eternal sleep for Kongzi. The Grave of Kongzi is known as the soul of Kong Forest.

After passing the observation tower, you'll catch sight of a small river flowing from east to west through Kong Forest. This is none other than the famous Zhushui River. It was built by man in the Zhou Dynasty to drain off floodwater and safeguard the city. As it passed by the Grave of Kongzi, the river was called the sacred river as it was believed its endless flow of water would last forever.

Of the three bridges spanning the Zhushui River, the middle one is a single arch bridge called Zhushui Bridge. The other two are ordinary flat bridges.

To the north of Zhushui Bridge is a three-bay gate covered with green tiles standing on a high platform. This is the gate of the sacred way leading to the Grave of Kongzi. There are nine steps before and nine steps beyond the gate. The two red-painted doors are inlaid with 81 decorative flower-patterned nails. This demonstrated the Greatest Sage's place of eternal sleep and also symbolized the dignity and prestige of Kongzi.

When you enter this gate, you'll see sacrificial halls and carved stones. The carved stones include stone figures, stone animals and ornamental columns erected before the grave. Stone figures act as guards or servants. Stone animals which can exorcize evil

A Distant View of Dry Riverbed of the Zhushui River and the Zhushui Bridge

Stone Animals and Statues of Wengzhong on Both Sides of the Path Leading to the Sacrificial Hall

spirits symbolize good luck. The carved stones stand for a kind of deterrent force, a special means adopted by the deceased to express his dignity to the living. The custom of placing carved stones in front of the grave started in the Eastern Han Dynasty.

Of all the carved stones in Kong Forest, those lining the sacred way in front of the sacrificial halls are the earliest set erected in 1123 (the 5th year of the reign of Emperor Xuanhe of the Song Dynasty). This set is composed of a pair of ornamental columns, a pair carved in the shape of *wenbao*, a pair in the shape of *jiaoduan* and a pair carved to resemble Wengzhong. The ornamental columns serve as a landmark to highlight the

Tombstones in Front of the Sacrificial Hall

threshold of the "heaven gate". *Wenbao* and *jiaoduan* are legendary animals used to protect the grave. Wengzhong was a valiant general of the Qin Dynasty who achieved miraculous feats in battles against Xiongnu. In order to make the two bronze or stone figures symmetrical, people created two personifications of Wengzhong—a civil official and a military general—to guard Kongzi's grave.

Affection of Kongzi and His Son and Grandson

Further to the north, there is a courtyard surrounded by a red-brick wall. This nuclear area of Kong Forest lies to the south of centre. Only Kongzi, his son Kong Li and his grandson Kong Ji are buried in this courtyard. All his other offspring are buried behind or on both sides of the courtyard according to the burial system of ancient China.

After passing the side door on the east side of the sacrificial hall, you'll step into the courtyard. Kongzi's grave lies towards the rear of the courtyard with his son Kong Li's grave on its east side, and his grandson Kong Ji's grave in front of it. The layout of graves like this is described as "a man bringing along his son and holding in his arms his grandson".

Stop-Over Pavilions

When you pay homage to Kongzi's grave, you'll be attracted by three ancient pavilions in line on the east side of the path. These pavilions are called the "stop-over pavilions" to honour emperors' trips to offer sacrifices to Kongzi. These four-pillar square pavilions were all built in the Qing Dynasty.

The south one is the stop-over pavilion in honour of Emperor Qianlong. The pavilion was built on a four-step-high terrace and covered with yellow glazed tiles. Emperor Qianlong paid homage to Kongzi several times and he rested in this pavilion every time he visited Kong Forest. The middle one was also built on a four-step-high terrace and covered with yellow glazed tiles. A stone tablet was erected in the pavilion to commemorate Emperor Kangxi's visit. In 1684 (the 23rd year of the reign of Emperor Kangxi), Emperor Kangxi came to Qufu and offered sacrifices to Kongzi at Kong Forest. He approved

Sacred Way behind the Sacrificial Hall

Grave of Kongzi in the Shadow of Old Cypresses

the Duke of Yansheng Kong Yuyin's request to expand the woodland. In commemoration of the imperial favour, they built the pavilion and erected the stone tablet. The north one was built in honour of Emperor Zhenzong of the Song Dynasty. The pavilion was built on a three-step-high terrace and covered with green glazed tiles. A stone tablet was erected to commemorate Emperor Zhenzong's visit. During his visit, he offered sacrifices to Kongzi and conferred the title of "greatest sage and prince of Wenxuan".

The Grave of Kongzi

If you turn west from the north pavilion, you'll arrive at Kongzi's grave. Kongzi was buried here after he passed away in 479 BC (the 16th year

Pavilion of Emperor Qianlong's Handwriting and Lined Cypresses

of the reign of Duke of Ai of the Lu Kingdom). The graveyard at this time covered an area of about seven hectares. According to historical records, the First Emperor of the Qin Dynasty once robbed Kongzi's gave. Kongzi's grave as we see it in the present day is 30 metres long from east to west, 28 metres wide from north to south and 5 metres high. Two tombstones stand in front of the grave. The rear tombstone was erected by the Duke of Yansheng Kong Yuancuo, Kongzi's descendant of the 51st generation and was inscribed with the words "Xuan Sheng Mu" (the tomb of Xuan Sage). The front tombstone was erected by Kong Yanjin, the Duke of Yansheng, Kongzi's descendant of the 59th generation and was inscribed with the words "Dacheng Zhisheng Wenxuan Wang Mu" (the tomb of Accomplished Sage Prince Wenxuan in the handwriting of Huang Yangzheng, a great calligrapher of the Ming Dynasty. In front of the tombstone there is a stone incense burner and an altar table made from piled up Taishan stones. After the death of Kongzi, his honorific titles were upgraded from dynasty to dynasty. The honorific titles "xuan sheng" and "dacheng zhisheng wenxuan wang" are two examples.

The Grave of Kong Li

The grave of Kong Li, which lies five metres to the east of Kongzi's grave, is 18 metres wide from east to west, 23 metres long from north to south and 3 metres high. Again, two tombstones stand in front of the grave. The rear tombstone was erected by the Duke of Yansheng Kong Yuancuo, Kongzi's descendant of the 51st generation and was inscribed with the words "the tomb of the second-generation ancestor". The front tombstone was set up by the Duke of Yansheng Kong Yanjin, Kongzi's descendant of the 59th generation and was inscribed with the words "the tomb of the Marquis of Sishui". In front of the tombstone there is a stone altar table, a stone incense burner and a brick platform upon which to kneel.

When Kong Li was born, the Duke of Zhao of the Lu Kingdom sent a carp ("li yu") to Kongzi as a congratulatory gift upon the birth of his son. Kongzi was so honoured that he gave the name "Li" (carp) to his newly-born son, and also called him "bo yu" (fish). Unfortunately, Kong Li died before Kongzi himself passed away. Kong Li was buried here; his grave later joined by his father's. The title of "the Marquis of Sishui" was conferred posthumously on him in 1102 (the first year of the reign of Emperor Chongning).

The Grave of Kong Ji

The grave of Kong Ji, which lies 20 metres to the south of the grave of Kongzi, is 18 metres wide from east to west, 21 metres long from north to south and is four metres high. Two tombstones stand in front of the grave. The rear tombstone was erected by the Duke of Yansheng Kong Yuancuo, Kongzi's descendant of the 51st generation and was inscribed with the words "the tomb of the third-generation ancestor". The front tombstone was set up by the Duke of Yansheng Kong Yanjin, Kongzi's descendant of the 59th generation and was inscribed with the words "the tomb of yi guo shu sheng gong (the Duke of Shusheng of the Yi Kingdom)". In front of the tombstone there is a stone altar table made in the Ming Dynasty. Further ahead a pair of plain-looking, though true to life, stone carvings of Wengzhong stand facing one another. This pair of Wengzhong carvings were originally made in the period of Xuanhe of the Northern Song Dynasty and placed on either side of the sacred way in front of the sacrificial hall. They were moved here in the 10th year of the reign of Emperor Yongzheng.

As a bright and clever boy, Kong Ji, courtesy name Zisi, was Kongzi's favourite grandson. We can learn from the book *Kong Cong Zi*, which records many conversations between Kongzi and his grandson, that Kongzi had high hopes for Kong Ji. While he was still quite young, Kong Ji was so influenced by Kongzi that he deemed it his responsibility to carry forward Kongzi's doctrines.

Kong Ji, or Zisi, was an important disciple of Kongzi's. He, his senior Zeng Shen and his junior Mengzi are all eminent Confucian scholars. The title of "the Marquis of Yishui" was conferred posthumously on him during the reign of Emperor Huizong of the Northern Song Dynasty. The title of "the Duke of Shusheng of the Yi Kingdom" was granted to him in the Yuan Dynasty. That's why Kong Ji was called "shusheng" by the people of later ages.

Left: Grave of Kong Ji

Place Where Zigong Kept Vigil

Zigong Keeps Vigil beside the Grave of Kongzi

In ancient times, children were required to be in mourning for the death of their father for three years. After Kongzi passed away, his disciples were also in heartfelt mourning over the death of their teacher for three years. Unlike Kongzi's children, who had to be dressed in white and with burlap draped over their shoulders, they were in mourning at heart only. Three years later, all Kongzi's disciples except Zigong bade farewell to Kongzi's grave and parted in tears. Zigong put up a shed near Kongzi's grave and spent another three years keeping vigil. In this way he expressed his fond

Three-Year Mourning

The three-year mourning is a kind of deep mourning observed by the son over the death of his father, the wife and concubine over their husband and the unmarried daughter over her father. During the three years, the mourners are required to wear mourning apparel and stop all recreational activities.

memories of and high regard for his esteemed teacher. In order to commemorate Zigong's boundless respect for his teacher, the imperial censor Chen Fengwu took charge of the construction of a three-room house to the west of the Grave of Kongzi to mark this event. A stone tablet was erected with the inscription "place where Zigong kept vigil". This grey-tiled house and the Chinese pistachio planted by Zigong are a historical witness to the relationship between Kongzi and his student which was as intimate as that between father and son. Zigong's noble act, showing respect for his teacher, has been held in esteem for thousands of years.

Place Where Zisi Wrote *The Doctrine of the Mean*

Famous Graves—from the Ancestor of Resurgence Kong Renyu to the First Duke of Yansheng

During the 2000 years since the death of Kongzi, his descendants have followed Kongzi in choosing Kong Forest as their place of eternal sleep. Due to the great number of his descendants and the limited space of

Group of Graves of the Ming Dynasty in Kong Forest

Kong Forest, their tombs were built close to each other, and even, in some cases, one upon the other. Except the graves of Kongzi, his son Kong Li, grandson Kong Ji and great grandson Kong Bai, the graves of all his other offspring until the 42nd generation were not marked. Starting from the 55th generation, his descendants had tombstones established before their graves. The graves of the Dukes of Yansheng after the middle period of the Ming Dynasty were decorated with carved stones. In front of some graves even stone gates and archways were set up. The graves of Kongzi's descendants who held a position as a cabinet minister or an even higher position were also decorated with carved stones.

More than 100,000 graves in Kong Forest can be divided into five groups: 1) the graves of Kongzi, his son and his grandson and the group of graves of the Period of the Warring States; 2) the group of graves of the Han Dynasty to the northwest and northeast of Kongzi's grave; 3) the group of graves of the Tang, Song and Jin Dynasties to the west and north of Kongzi's grave; 4) the group of graves of the Yuan and Ming Dynasties in the west and northwest parts of Kong Forest; and 5) the group of graves of the Qing Dynasty and modern day in the northeast part of Kong Forest. Many of those buried here were famous personages while alive and were well remembered by people of later ages after their deaths. When you tour Kong Forest, you'll find the graves of those you are interested in.

The Grave of Kong Renyu, the Ancestor of Resurgence

About 100 metres away from the northeast wall of the courtyard where the Grave of Kongzi is situated, there is a middle-sized four-chamber brick grave with a stone tablet erected in front. This is the grave of Kong Renyu, Kongzi's descendant of the 43rd generation. He was commended by the younger generations of the Kong clan as the "ancestor of resurgence".

When he was nine months old, his father, Kong Guangsi, was murdered by a servant named Kong Mo. Kong Mo passed himself off as a descendant of Kongzi's and assumed the position of Magistrate of Qufu. As he was hidden in the house of Madame Zhang (his maternal grandmother), Kong Renyu wasn't killed by Kong Mo. He changed his name and was brought up by the Zhang family. During the reign of Emperor Mingzong of the Tang

Relics of the Graves of the Han Dynasty in Kong Forest

Dynasty, somebody submitted a memorandum to the emperor, revealing the truth of Kong Mo's scheme. The emperor issued an imperial edict to execute Kong Mo and restored Kong Renyu to the post of Magistrate of Qufu in charge of all the sacrificial rites in memory of Kongzi. The title of "the Duke of Wenxuan" was conferred on him. After his death, he was granted the rank of the Minister of War.

Thanks to Kong Renyu, the Kong clan was rescued from a desperate situation and its members multiplied into "five branches", "20 groups" and "60 households" in succession. Kong Renyu's posterity respectfully called him "the ancestor of resurgence". In addition to offering sacrifices to Kongzi, his son and his grandson in their family temple, the Kong clansmen also pay homage to Kong Renyu. This demonstrates how Kong Renyu was held in great esteem by his descendants.

Portrait of Kong Renyu

The Grave of Kong Zongyuan, the First Duke of Yansheng

About 50 metres away from the west wall of the courtyard where the Grave of Kongzi is situated, there is a medium-sized grave with two stone tablets erected in front. This is the grave of the first Duke of Yansheng Kong Zongyuan, Kongzi's descendant of the 46th generation.

Kong Zongyuan, courtesy name Zizhuang, strictly followed the teachings of his ancestors and studied very diligently when he was a boy. During the reign of Emperor Renzong of the Song Dynasty he obtained his first official position. The Duke of Wenxuan Kong Shengyou died and had no son to inherit his title "the Duke of Wenxuan". Emperor Renzong issued an imperial edict to confer the title on Kong Shenyou's cousin Kong Zongyuan and

appointed him Director of the Imperial Academy and the Magistrate of Qufu. While in office, Kong Zongyuan presented a petition to the emperor. With the emperor's approval, he expanded the ancestral hall in the Kong Temple in Mount Nishan and founded a school there. This was the embryonic form of Nishan Academy of Classical Learning. In 1055 Emperor Renzong of the Song Dynasty changed his title from "the Duke of Wenxuan" to "the Duke of Yansheng". Since then, the title of "the Duke of Yansheng" has been conferred on 41 descendants of Kongzi's from 32 generations over 880 years across the Song, Jin, Yuan, Ming and Qing Dynasties and the Republic of China. In

The Page Depicting How the Title of the Duke Yansheng Was Conferred on Kong Zongyuan

Tombstone of the First Duke of Yansheng Kong Zongyuan

1935 (the 24th year of the Republic of China) Kong Decheng, Kongzi's descendant of the 77th generation, was granted the title of "the official in charge of sacrificial rites in memory of the greatest sage and teacher" instead of "the Duke of Yansheng". As a rule, every Duke of Yansheng was buried with special honours.

Situated to the southwest of Kongzi's grave is the group of graves of the Song Dynasty. Kong Fan, Kongzi's descendant of the 49th generation, was buried here. Kong Fan, courtesy name Wenlao, was born in 1103 (the 2nd year of the reign of Emperor Huizong of the Song Dynasty). After the Jin Dynasty conquered the Northern Song Dynasty, Emperor Gaozong of the Southern Song Dynasty ordered the Duke of Yansheng Kong Duanyou to come to the south and assist in presiding over a sacrificial rite. The ruler of the Jin Dynasty also showed respect to Kongzi and Confucianism. He ordered Kong Duanyou's younger brother Kong Duancao to inherit the title of the Duke of Yansheng and take charge of sacrificial rites held in Qufu. After Kong Duancao died, his son Kong Fan became the first official Duke of Yansheng of the northern branch of the Kong clan. He died in 1142 (the 2nd year of the reign of Emperor Huangtong of the Jin Dynasty) and was granted the title of a senior official.

The Graves of Some Famous Personages of the Kong Family from the Qing Dynasty

In the group of graves of the Qing Dynasty some famous personages are worth our visiting and remembering.

The Grave of Kong Xianpei

Located one kilometre away to the northeast of the grave of Kongzi is an eye-catching exquisitely carved wooden memorial arch. This four-pillar three-layered arch is decorated with colourful painted patterns on a blue and green background. It was built in 1825 (the fifth year of the reign of Emperor Daoguang of the Qing Dynasty), when an imperial envoy sent by the emperor came to offer sacrifices to Madame Yu, the mother of the Duke of Yansheng Kong Qingrong. The front side of the memorial arch was carved with the imperial edict issued by Emperor Daoguang praising her exemplary conduct and virtue. The rear side was inscribed with four golden characters "luan yin bao de" (paragon of virtue), so this memorial arch is called the "Luanyin Baode Memorial Arch". Kong Xianpei and his wife Madame Yu were buried together in the grave behind the memorial arch.

Madame Yu was the wife of the Duke of Yansheng Kong Xianpei, Kongzi's descendant of the 72nd generation and the adoptive daughter of Yu Minzhong, Secretary of the Grand Council and Minister of Revenue. Tradition has it that she was the daughter of Emperor Qianlong. Emperor Qianlong liked very much the Duke of Yansheng Kong Xianyun and thought he was a very promising young man. The emperor decided to change his name from Kong Xianyun to Kong Xianpei and betroth his daughter to him. Unfortunately, Madame Yu did not give birth to

Luanyin Baode Memorial Arch

any children. Therefore, when Kong Xianpei died, the title of the Duke of Yansheng was inherited by his younger brother's eldest son, Kong Qingrong.

Kong Qingrong showed great respect to Madame Yu. After Madame Yu died, Kong Qingrong erected a memorial arch for her in Kong Forest and built the five-room Mu'en Hall in the east courtyard of Kong Residence. The Mu'en Hall was decorated with the portraits of Kong Xianpei and Madame Yu, an ancestral tablet, a wooden carving of the sitting couple facing each other and a painting of the couple enjoying their life. Of all the wives of the Dukes of Yansheng, only Madame Yu enjoyed the privileges of having an ancestral hall built for her in Kong

Residence and a memorial arch established for her in Kong Forest. The stone figures, horses and ornamental column standing in front of the grave of Kong Xianpei were the most spectacular among all the graves of the Dukes of Yansheng.

The Grave of Kong Shangren

In the rear part of Kong Forest and to the north of the ring road stands a large grave. This is the grave of Kong Shangren, a famous dramatist in the Qing Dynasty.

Kong Shangren, courtesy name Dongtang or An'tang, was Kongzi's descendant of the 64th generation. He was born into a family of scholars—his grandfather being a student of a prefectural school and his father being a successful candidate who passed the imperial examination at the provincial level. Kong Shangren was well educated when he was young, but unfortunately, he never passed the imperial examinations. He made determined efforts to better himself by living and studying in seclusion at Shimen Mountain. As he was learned and well-informed about rites and music and was invited in 1864 (the 20th year of the reign of Emperor Kangxi) by the Duke of Yansheng Kong Yuyin to help with the domestic affairs of the Duke of Yansheng Residence. Enjoying the trust of Kong Yuyin, Kong Shangren devoted himself to compiling the genealogy of

Peach Blossom Fan

Peach Blossom Fan was adopted as the motif for the play of the love story between Hou Fangyu, a scholar of the Fu Society and Li Xiangjun, a famous prostitute along the Yangtze-Huaihe Valley. The play aimed to depict the social unrest in the latter periods of the Ming Dynasty. The sad story of partings and reunions was used to express the author's concern about the fate of the nation. The play was performed by many theatrical troupes and caused a great sensation in the capital.

Grave of Kong Shangren

the Kong clan and supervising the repair of musical instruments and sacrificial vessels. When Emperor Kangxi made an inspection tour to Qufu, Kong Shangren served as the emperor's guide during his visit to Kong Temple and Kong Forest. He and Kong Shangli were ordered to lecture on Confucianism in front of the emperor. Satisfied with his lecture, Emperor Kangxi made an exception and conferred on him the title of the "Specialist of the Imperial College". This was the beginning of his official career.

While in office, Kong Shangren became acquainted with some former officials of the Ming Dynasty. He was so affected by the fall of the Ming Dynasty that he took great pains to write a legendary play *Peach Blossom Fan* after writing three initial drafts. After reading the play, Emperor Kangxi sensed Kong Shangren's grudge against the Qing Dynasty and found a pretext for removing him from office. Kong Shangren left the capital for his hometown and dwelled in seclusion again in the picturesque Shimen Mountain until his death.

The Grave of Kong Lingyi

Kong Lingyi, courtesy name Yanting, was Kongzi's descendant of the 76th generation. He was granted the title of the Duke of Yansheng in 1877 (the third year of the reign of Emperor Guangxu of the Qing Dynasty). His grave lies to the east of the ring road. The stone tablet in front of his grave is decorated with the carved patterns of wheat heads and dragons. You can find before the tablet a carved stone altar table and a stone tripod. The stone figures, animals and ornamental column were set up by his daughter Kong Demao.

While taking a stroll in Kong Forest, you'll find yourself amidst towering ancient trees, numerous stone tablets and groups of stone ornaments. This is an exhibition of ancient Chinese grave culture as well as a natural botanical garden. You'll be fascinated by the changing scenes and sights in different seasons.

Kong Temple, Kong Residence and Kong Forest combine to form a sacred place of traditional Chinese culture. By taking a tour of this sacred place, you will enjoy a splendid passage through the long history of China. You will travel from the source of Chinese history and culture over 2500 years ago to the present-day Qufu of the 21st century. With the rapid development of the world, Qufu undergoes changes day by day. Just as Kongzi once asked, "Is it not a great pleasure to have friends coming from afar?" this city of ancient culture welcomes visitors from all over the world.

Epilogue

We have lived in Kongzi's hometown our whole lives and were nurtured in the spirit of Confucianism. But still, we found our ability was not equal to the task of writing an introductory book about the sacred place of Kongzi.

After I was entrusted by Mr. Wang Lixiang with the task of writing this book, I started to make an outline of the book, work out its layout and prepare a draft. I also took into consideration the maps, notes and illustrations to be attached to the book.

Being pressed for time, I invited my colleagues Liu Shuqiang, Kong Deli and Zhou Haisheng to write the chapters on Kong Temple, Kong Residence and Kong Forest respectively. I was responsible for revising their first drafts. Not completely satisfied with the writing style, I asked Mr. Wang Hua to revise and polish their drafts. He not only excels at writing beautifully, he is also well-learned and quick on the uptake. He often worked long hours of overtime in the name of this book. He spared no effort to revise the whole book, and even to rewrite some sections.

Mr. Wang Lixiang gave detailed instructions and Mr. Luo Hao, the editor in charge of the Chinese edition, was meticulous about the details of writing. Kong Deli did a good job in supplementing pictures.

This book of moderate length is the painstaking effort of the whole team. I am grateful to all of them.

Yang Zhaoming

At the Lantern Festival of 2004

Dynasties in Chinese History

Xia Dynasty	c.2070BC – c.1600BC
Shang Dynasty	c.1600BC – c.1046BC
Zhou Dynasty	c.1046BC – c.221BC
Western Zhou Dynasty	c.1046BC – c.771BC
Eastern Zhou Dynasty	770BC – 256BC
Spring and Autumn Period	770BC – 476BC
Warring States Period	475BC – 221BC
Qin Dynasty	221BC – 206BC
Han Dynasty	206BC – 220AD
Western Han Dynasty	206BC – 25AD
Eastern Han Dynasty	25AD – 220AD
Three Kingdoms	220AD – 280AD
Wei	220AD – 265AD
Shu Han	221AD – 263AD
Wu	222AD – 280AD
Jin Dynasty	265AD – 420AD
Western Jin Dynasty	265AD – 316AD
Eastern Jin Dynasty	317AD – 420AD
Northern and Southern Dynasties	420AD – 589AD
Southern Dynasties	420AD – 589AD
Northern Dynasties	439AD – 581AD
Sui Dynasty	581AD – 618AD
Tang Dynasty	618AD – 907AD
Five Dynastives and Ten States	907AD – 960AD
Five Dynasties	907AD – 960AD
Ten States	902AD – 979AD
Song Dynasty	960AD – 1279AD
Northern Song Dynasty	960AD – 1127AD
Southern Song Dynasty	1127AD – 1279AD
Liao Dynasty	907AD – 1125AD
Jin Dynasty	1115AD – 1234AD
Xixia Dynasty	1038AD – 1227AD
Yuan Dynasty	1279AD – 1368AD
Ming Dynasty	1368AD – 1644AD
Qing Dynasty	1644AD – 1911AD